AGAINST INCLUSION

Tyranny In The Name Of Diversity

Amardo Rodriguez

ISBN-13: 9780692043189 (Public Square Press)
ISBN-10: 0692043187

LCCN Imprint Name:

Public Square Press
102 Palmer Drive
Fayetteville, NY 13066
USA

Dedicated to the members of Theta Tau, Syracuse University Chapter

Whenever you find yourself on the side of the majority,
it is time to pause and reflect.

Mark Twain

CONTENTS

Prologue ix

Chapter 1   Making Inclusion and Diversity Policy   1
Chapter 2   Notes on an Inclusion Affair   15
Chapter 3   Problems with Language Politics   45
Chapter 4   Diversity, Inclusion & Harm   66
Chapter 5   Diversity Versus Inclusion   90
Chapter 6   Inclusion is an Abstraction   99
Chapter 7   Inclusion Delusions   112
Chapter 8   Beyond Inclusion   133

Epilogue   145
References   149
About the Author   155

PROLOGUE

We remain determined to bridge our differences, accommodate our differences, include our differences. For us, inclusion is moral. It is inherently good. It supposedly gives us unity, stability, and prosperity, thus saving us from trouble and strife. It also supposedly allows us to harness each other's differences, thereby promoting learning and innovation.

But in this book I argue against inclusion. Rather than promoting diversity, I contend that inclusion diminishes human diversity, brutalizes human diversity, and, ultimately, destroys human diversity. Nothing about inclusion is good for human diversity. Inclusion assumes that in order for us to thrive collectively, our differences must be tamed, sanitized, and harmonized. Inclusion must come first, meaning that diversity must always yield to the demands of inclusion. However, in destroying diversity, inclusion protects the status quo by promoting conformity and homogeneity. The diversity that inclusion champions is nothing but a caricature of diversity. It is diversity in name only. It has no capacity or yearning to disrupt or renew anything. Its only ambition is to be included and affirmed.

In this book I treat inclusion as a hegemon—a vast system of values, beliefs, fears, structures, and practices that imposes and sustains a certain set of supposed truths about the human experience. Nearly every institution now has many departments, such as an Office of Equal Opportunity, Inclusion and Resolution Services, many administrative positions, such as a Chief Diversity Officer, courses, workshops, regulations, committees, such as a Council on Diversity and Inclusion, and Diversity and Inclusion grants, all dedicated to promoting diversity and inclusion. I aim to demystify this hegemon, specifically the implications and consequences that come with this hegemon. In the first chapter I use a case study, the first of many, to look at how inclusion and diversity policy is constructed, instituted, and imposed upon us as something that is both necessary and good. In the second chapter I show how inclusion and diversity policy work institutionally to destroy diversity by suppressing communication. In the third chapter I look at the integral role that language politics (e.g., speech codes, trigger warnings, language covenants, microaggressions, hate speech laws) play in impoverishing communication and, consequently, undermining democracy, which I contend is vital for the flourishing of human diversity. In fact, without language politics, inclusion is nothing. Language politics is the military wing of inclusion. It is diversity thuggery—using force and violence in the name of diversity to achieve homogeneity.

I contend that language politics is all delusions and falsehoods. It has no foundation in either science or history. I also contend that its thuggery encourages cruelty, and ultimately promotes homogeneity rather than diversity. In the fourth chapter I look at the notion of harm, such as the claim that certain words, phrases, and ideas need to be institutionally suppressed for the sake of achieving inclusion because they supposedly cause harm and hurt to minority peoples. In the fifth chapter I look at how inclusion sets various discursive forces and practices in motion that make human diversity impossible. I specifically look at the insidious ways inclusion flattens out our differences by suppressing communication. In the sixth chapter I look at how inclusion trades in abstractions that ultimately promote our own alienation and separation from ourselves and each other. In the seventh chapter I discuss how institutions, for the sake of preserving order, conformity, and continuity, reduce diversity to plurality, and pass off plurality as diversity. I use different examples in communication studies to show how plurality works insidiously to suppress diversity. In the final chapter I look beyond inclusion and towards a world that genuinely values human diversity in all its infinite forms and expressions because of its vital role in human flourishing.

That I am against inclusion in no way means that I am against diversity. This is no colorblind book. I am against inclusion because it destroys human diversity for the sake of preserving the status quo. Also, that I am against inclusion in no way means that I support exclusion and know nothing of the brutality, cruelty, and inequality that marginalized and disenfranchised peoples constantly face. I will always side first with the marginalized, the downtrodden, and the forsaken. The reason being, "the personal is political." Yet history teaches that exile and exclusion play a vital role in nurturing human diversity. Nearly all of our icons and prophets came from places of exile and exclusion. I prefer to view inclusion/exclusion dialectically rather than oppositionally. Finally, that I am against inclusion in no way means that I am against history, meaning the enduring and torturous legacy of over 350 years of slavery, Black codes, Jim Crow, and all other kinds of oppression against African Americans, Native Americans, Asians, women, immigrants, and peoples of different kinds of sexual orientations. I am against inclusion because it represents an impoverished and disingenuous reckoning with this history. After all, what discussion of inclusion makes any mention of the word reparations? In my view, history demands something much larger and better than inclusion. For why should the ancestors of any history of oppression, discrimination, and exploitation want to be included in the same kind of systems and arrangements that remain hostile to human flourishing in all its infinite forms and expression?

Inclusion rises by vanquishing communication. Inclusion trades in nouns and groupings, whereas communication is about verbs and processes. Through communication nothing remains the same. That is, through communication our meanings change, our perspectives change, our interpretations change, our understandings change, our truths change, our conceptions of ourselves change, and our views of others change. Through communication there is always the possibility for something new to appear and change us. In this way, communication undermines inclusion by undermining all of the stereotyping and homogenizing that inclusion needs to succeed. Communication is the antithesis of inclusion. In order for human diversity to rise, communication must flourish, which means that communication and inclusion hold to fundamentally different definitions of diversity. Instead of residing within groups, labels, and boxes, human diversity resides within communication, and thus between us rather than within us. It is ecological rather than individual, relational rather than personal. That human beings must evolve and change in order to survive and thrive means that our diversity must also change and evolve. Diversity is something we become rather than something we are. I develop this thesis throughout this book.

CHAPTER 1
MAKING INCLUSION AND DIVERSITY POLICY

N early every college and university in the United States has a formal diversity and inclusion policy that aims to promote diversity and inclusion by prohibiting practices and behaviors that supposedly undercut such goals. Below are excerpts from Syracuse University's policy, which likely resembles every other policy at every other university in the US. It is titled *Building a Culture of Respect, Diversity and Inclusion* and begins with listing the university's core principles.

Syracuse University's Core Principles:

The Code of Ethical Conduct is a statement of principles guiding the activities of all faculty, staff, and students. It provides, in part:

- *We respect the rights and dignity of all persons and recognize that discrimination or harassment in any form undermines the fundamental principles of the University.*
- *We support a respectful environment through our own actions, encourage respectful behavior in others, and speak out against hatred and bias.*

1

Students at Syracuse University are expected to conduct themselves in a manner supportive of the educational mission of the institution. Integrity, respect for the person and property of others and a commitment to intellectual and personal growth in a diverse population are values deemed fundamental to membership in this University community.

Much of what comes to the Equal Opportunity, Inclusion and Resolution Services office are issues arising out of a failure to collaborate—a failure of team work. People feel isolated, unsupported, detached, not listened to, unimportant, marginalized.

Be aware of micro-inequities such as interrupting a person not of the dominant group; validating the ideas of people from the dominant group and ignoring the ideas of others; or otherwise overlooking, ignoring, discounting or singling out women and people of color. Micro-inequities are not only destructive of the team but can leave a person feeling marginalized because of age, race, gender, sexual orientation, national origin or because of any other protected category.

Think and act as a team: committed to a common purpose and each other and generating synergy through people helping each other, coordinating their efforts, maximizing individual strengths, and contributing consistent with their strengths.

Behaviors that may create a hostile environment:

- *Verbal/audible (jokes, teasing, nicknames, suggestive remarks, flirting, sexual advances, music with graphic lyrics, etc.)*
- *Non-verbal (gestures, leering)*
- *Other visual (graphic pictures, screen savers, email jokes, text messages, cards, etc.)*

- *Derogatory comments about or descriptions of a someone that implicates race, disability, gender, sex, sexual orientation and any other protected category.*
- *Physical and/or mental bullying and/or intimidating behavior. Abuse of power is a theme in cases against people in power. The path to abuse of power may be paved with:*

  - *Singling out an individual for special, personal attention*
  - *Using rewards and punishments to establish control*
  - *Publicly or privately humiliating an individual/using guilt*
  - *Indicating that an individual is the chosen, or elite, possibly belittling peers*
  - *Encouraging secretiveness about interactions between them*
  - *Making comments about sexual likes and dislikes*
  - *Fostering a strong sense of dependence/indebtedness*

Welcome v. Unwelcome

- *Complainant has no legal obligation to express discomfort with the behavior or to tell the person to stop or to have filed any kind of internal complaint.*
- *The Complainant may have even appeared to go along with behavior such as laughing and joking along with the others.*
- *To tolerate something or to consent to something does not mean it is welcome.*

Intent v. Impact

- *Whether harassment has occurred is determined by the impact on the Complainant and not by the intent of the harasser.*
- *"I was only joking"; "I did not mean to offend"; "I thought it was ok"; "I thought it was all just in good fun" are not legal defenses.*

Responsibilities:

- *Don't do or say anything that could be perceived as harassing.*
- *If you are comfortable doing so, intervene when you hear any comments or observe any conduct between others (such as between students, a faculty member or a third party) that could be perceived as harassing.*
- *When a person comes to you with a concern, listen carefully and without judgment or defensiveness when a person voices a concern (need not be in writing).*
- *When possible, provide complainant with information sheet summarizing University policies, providing key definitions, specifying complainant's rights, options and resources.*

Positive Steps to Prevent Harassment

- *Model appropriate behavior.*
- *Ensure that others are aware of our policies.*
- *Do a friend a favor – talk with him/her if they're in danger of violating a policy.*
- *Ask yourself – would you say/do it if your spouse, son, daughter, supervisor, etc. were in the room?*
- *Would you write it if your spouse, son, daughter, supervisor, etc. could read your email?*
- *Would you do this or say this if it was going to be on the news later today?*
- *Can you prove that your behavior is welcome? Never assume that jokes or other comments or conduct related to any protected category are welcome.*
- *Understand that no communication is anonymous.*
- *Report problems to the Title IX Coordinator (443.0211) if it happens to you or if you see or hear about it happening to others.*

But our goal is not merely compliance. Remember our Code of Ethical Conduct:

- *We respect the rights and dignity of all persons and recognize that discrimination or harassment in any form undermines the fundamental principles of the University.*
- *We support a respectful environment through our own actions, encourage respectful behavior in others, and speak out against hatred and bias.*

Enter the Problems

Putting aside the fact that nearly every college and university in the United States is legally obligated to have and enforce these kinds of diversity and inclusion policies, the reasons for these policies are no doubt well-intentioned, especially in a country with a sordid history of brutalizing, marginalizing, and discriminating against all kinds of minority peoples. However, these policies begin on assumptions that undermine rather than promote human diversity. Nowhere is this more evident than in how communication is assumed and defined.

Syracuse University's diversity and inclusion policy assumes that communication is about language and symbols, and that meaning resides in language and symbols. Consequently, the policy focuses on the *impact* of communication. Supposedly, negative language and symbols make for negative emotions and situations. Again, sections in Syracuse University's policy read, "Complainant has no legal obligation to express discomfort with the behavior or to tell the person to stop or to have filed any kind of . . . complaint. The Complainant may have even appeared to go along with behavior such as laughing and joking along with the others. To tolerate something or to consent to something does not mean it is welcome." In fact, "Whether harassment has occurred is determined by the impact on the Complainant and not by the intent of the harasser. "I was only joking"; "I did not mean to offend"; "I thought it was ok"; "I thought it was all just in good fun" are not legal defenses. However, without the aggrieved person providing feedback to the person who is supposedly doing the offending, and even being released from providing feedback, which is an important element in many scholarly models of communication, how is any person to know someone is being hurt and offended, and thus to know when to stop saying or doing something, especially when the complainant is going along with the behavior by "laughing and joking along with the others"? Moreover, how could intent constitute no defense? In a world of boundless human diversity, meaning one where even members of a supposed homogenous group barely share anything, how is anyone to know exactly or even reliably what any other person finds to be offensive and hurtful without resorting to stereotyping?

Syracuse University's diversity and inclusion policy also assumes that communication is outside and separate from human diversity. But notions like *polysemy, polyphony,* and *heteroglossia*—different peoples sharing the same language but living differently in the language and also using the language to achieve different things—reveal that this assumption is false. In other words, to claim that certain words are inherently offensive is to assume that human diversity has nothing to do with how words are defined, judged, and experienced. However, language diversity is bound up with human diversity. The reality of different words meaning different things to different peoples— even to peoples of the same race, gender, nationality, and sexual orientation—reminds us that human diversity should always figure prominently in our understanding of things. No word or phrase is inherently offensive or derogatory. It is always a matter of *whom,* as in *who* is judging certain words and phrases to be offensive and derogatory, and *who* gets to dictate or impose such a reality on others?

Syracuse University's diversity and inclusion policy also assumes that context has nothing much to do with communication. But how could context play no important role in communication? Case in point, Syracuse University's policy ends with the following recommendation, "Don't do or say anything that could be perceived as harassing. If you are comfortable doing so, intervene when you hear any comments or observe any conduct between others . . . that could be perceived as harassing." But what constitutes "harassing" language has much to do with context. One person's harassing language could always be another person's honest language. It all depends on the context that the person is assuming is in play. Appreciating human diversity means recognizing that our meanings and interpretations can always be different because of our different backgrounds, circumstances, struggles, resources, and influences lending for different kinds of context. Consequently, context should matter in communication, and especially to persons who claim to value human diversity.

No Learning Please

A university is supposed to be a place of study, learning, and enlightenment. All of this begins on the premise that nothing should be assumed. Everything should be interrogated, and always from different perspectives. As such, how to explain the glaring lack of learning that pervades Syracuse University's diversity and inclusion policy? For instance,

I. What exactly is a "respectful environment"? Who defines and determines what is a "respectful environment"? Similarly, what exactly is "respectful behavior"? Who defines and determines what is "respectful behavior"? In short, which definitions of these concepts are outside of culture and ideology, and thus have nothing to do with power and privilege?

II. Why does being of a certain race, creed, gender, religion, or sexual orientation mean that a person is "in a position of vulnerability"? That is, why does being of a certain persuasion mean that I am in "a position of vulnerability" and thereby need certain protections from the university? Why is the university making this assumption about all members of minority groups? Did these persons give the university permission to do so? Indeed, "in whose interest is it to persuade [students] that they're fragile, that they're threatened, that words are violence, that an imagined slight is as bad as a real one, and that they're surrounded by people and ideas from whom they need so much protection?" (Asher, 2018).

III. Why should students be "expected to conduct themselves in a manner supportive of the educational mission of the institution," especially when they had no involvement in defining what this means? How and by what means were certain expectations determined to be supportive of learning, and which of these expectations have nothing to do with ideology and power? In short, what does conducting ourselves "in a manner supportive of the educational mission of the institution" mean and to whom?

IV. What are derogatory comments? Who determines what are derogatory comments, and why those persons rather than others? If nothing is outside of culture, and the goal of every diversity and inclusion policy is to promote, among other things, cultural diversity, then what persons should have the power to criticize the cultural norms of others?

V. What are the larger consequences of living in a world where neither our intentions nor motivations matter? If any person has the legal and institutional power to claim that our own behavior is derogatory and threatening, regardless of our intentions and motivations, what then becomes the possibility of controlling our own lives, especially when "I did not mean to offend" is no legal defense?

VI. Finally, what becomes the possibility of diversity when no person can "say anything that could be perceived as harassing"? What does such intimidation do for diversity, and how does the need for such conformity redeem any argument for diversity? Also, who, and by what authority, gets to define and determine what is "perceived as harassing"?

Syracuse University's diversity and inclusion policy assumes that conformity is necessary for diversity to thrive. We presumably promote diversity by being of the same values, beliefs, sentiments, and expectations, thereby uniformly agreeing on what is offensive language and behavior. But how could conformity promote diversity? Syracuse University's diversity and inclusion policy assumes that diversity must be coercively controlled and limited in order to achieve good things. Failure to do so will presumably result in chaos and minority peoples being harmed. But what is the foundation of this common assumption? What kind of science or evidence validates this assumption? What moment in history affirms this assumption? Moreover, how did inclusion become the goal we should value and promote, and why must diversity be included in order to thrive? Can diversity have no other ambitions? Indeed, the only diversity that conformity produces is a diversity that is ideologically and epistemologically depoliticized, a diversity that poses no threat to anything. Syracuse University's diversity and inclusion policy caricatures diversity. It reduces diversity to an object, something a person possesses by simply being of a certain racial, physical, and sexual persuasion. It assumes that diversity emerges by adding, including, and accommodating more of these peoples.

In the end, Syracuse University's diversity and inclusion policy undermines human diversity by forcing all of us to use language and symbols in ways that conform to a common sensibility, rationality, and modality. However, what becomes of human diversity when I must find offensive what you find to be offensive or else face sanction? Why must my sensibility conform to your sensibility? How did your sensibility come to be the sensibility of power and privilege, that is, the sensibility that dictates who is shamed and silenced? Moreover, Syracuse University's diversity and inclusion policy lessens the intensity and ferocity of communication, making only for the illusion of social, racial, and political progress. In short, this policy makes for a false civility. It succeeds by saving us from the tension that comes with dealing openly and honestly with our differences. We thereby never develop the temperament that is vital to navigating difficult and wrenching scenarios.

Conclusion

Syracuse University's diversity and inclusion policy reveals how inclusion rises by vanquishing communication. It wants nothing to do with communication. It is all rules and regulations, all for the sake of achieving conformity. It thrives on stereotyping and convincing us that group differences must trump human differences. In vanquishing communication, Syracuse University's policy vanquishes diversity. For only through communication we are able to recognize and appreciate how every human being, regardless of race, gender, nationality, ability, or sexual orientation, perceives and experiences the world differently as a result of being of different backgrounds, circumstances, resources, struggles, and influences. In other words, only through communication our diversity emerges, and everything that makes for our diversity. However, this is an unfolding diversity, a diversity that is always moving, changing, and becoming. This diversity is never one thing. It is also neither absolute nor complete. Communication is always changing us, just as how water changes the contours of a river as it moves down the river, and the changing contours in turn change the flow of the water. In a world of boundless ambiguity, one that is always demanding of us new meanings and interpretations, all that is constant is change.

Finally, Syracuse University's diversity and inclusion undermines human flourishing by discouraging us from taking responsibility for the condition of our lives. According to the *Thomas Theorem*, "If men define situations as real, they are real in their consequences." That is, the interpretation of a situation causes the action and reaction. As such, something is a problem only if you choose to make it a problem. In this case, certain words and symbols are a problem only if you choose to make either a problem. There is no law in the universe that determines certain words and symbols to be inherently offensive. This is purely our doing. In fact, even the notion of "offensive" is of our making as many cultures have no such notion. Also, you choosing to make certain words and symbols a problem should in no way obligate the rest of us to do likewise. If anything, human diversity should mean that you should respect my choice just as much as I should respect yours. Indeed, *choice theory*, a popular theory in psychology, would posit that claiming to find a word or phrase to be offensive is a choice. You have chosen to be angry and feel hurt in response to hearing a word. You have made a choice, and choices have consequences. However, you are by no means devoid of agency and thus purely a victim of language or how another person chooses to use language. You can always make better choices, and should be encouraged, at least by any university, to do so. As Don Miguel Ruiz explains in *The Four Agreements: A Toltec Wisdom Book*,

> When you take things personally, then you feel offended, and your reaction is to defend your beliefs and create conflict. You make something big out of something little, because you have the need to be right and make everybody else wrong. You also try hard to be right by giving your own

opinions. In the same way, whatever you feel and do is just projection of your own personal dream, a reflection of your own agreements. What you say, what you do, and the options you have are according to the agreements you have made—and these opinions have nothing to do with me.

Indeed, claiming that certain words, symbols, and phrases make you angry or harm you assumes that your response is natural and even proper. But as Marshall B. Rosenberg explains in *Nonviolent Communication: A Language of Life*, when "we are angry, we are finding fault—we are choosing to play God by judging or blaming the other person for being wrong or deserving of punishment." In other words, anger results from us releasing ourselves of being responsible for the condition of our own lives. It represents weakness, as in allowing ourselves to be controlled by our instincts and impulses, and thus being unwilling to look carefully and thoughtfully at the consequences of our actions and decisions.

Buddhism also gives us another way to understand how Syracuse University's diversity and inclusion undermines human flourishing by promoting egotism and narcissism. In Buddhism *The First Noble Truth* is that "There is suffering." To live is to suffer. The challenge is to avoid as much unnecessary suffering as possible, and deal constructively with any that remains. However, nearly all of our suffering is of our own making. As Yongey Mingyur Rinpoche, a prominent Tibetan Buddhist master, notes in *Joyful Wisdom: Embracing Change and Finding Freedom*, "Our normal tendency is to assign the cause of suffering to circumstances or conditions. . . . however, the cause of suffering lies not in events or circumstances, but in the way we perceive and interpret our experiences as it unfolds." We make our own suffering by viewing ourselves at the center of everything and thereby demanding that everything conforms to our wants, desires, aspirations, needs, and expectations. In other words, our suffering begins in our egotism and narcissism. Case in point, to profess to be outraged and offended by certain words and symbols is to demand that what you find to be offensive and hurtful should matter equally to the rest of world. But you are merely one human being on a planet with billions of human beings. What about all the many things that the rest of us on this planet find to be hurtful and offensive? Where is your outrage over the things that outrage us, such as the killing of animals to satisfy your meat consumption? Why should what you find to be offensive and hurtful be assumed to be more important than what the rest of us finds to be so? In fact, why should the rest of the world even care about what you find to be offensive and hurtful, especially when attending to your issues does nothing to relieve the misery and suffering that millions of other human beings are dealing with? How did you come to believe that you are so special, and why should the rest of us encourage your egotism and narcissism? What certain words mean to us is nothing but a creature of our own perspective of things. The same words and phrases can mean completely different things from different perspectives. Coming to terms with this reality is the beginning of human diversity. What matters in the end is our *perspective* of things rather than the supposed truth of things. As the Buddha teaches, "When the mind exists undisturbed in the Way, nothing in the world can offend, and when a thing can no longer offend, it ceases to exist in the old way."

Indeed, what Buddhism teaches about the origins of human misery is no way fundamentally different from what Stoicism teaches. Stoicism contends that our misery results from our own actions, specifically from our own perceptions and judgments of things and persons. Nothing outside of us inherently has the power to do anything to us. In the words of Marcus Aurelius (2006), "things in themselves have no inherent power to form our judgments" (p. 57). In being outside of us, "things cannot touch the mind" and thus torment it. Instead, the mind is vexed, angered, and tormented by things inside of us, specifically through our perceptions and judgments, which in turn are born from our thoughts. Thus, "Remove the judgment, and you have removed the thought 'I am hurt': remove the thought 'I am hurt', and the hurt itself is removed" (p. 25). Stoicism contends that we become susceptible to being controlled by outside things, what Marcus Aurelius refers to as "externals," when our minds are weak, that is, when we lack the ability to control our instincts, impulses, and desires. This is how we come to form perceptions and judgments that are destructive, such as falsely believing that the words of others have the power to harm and hurt us. When our minds become susceptible to outside things, we become emotional rather than rational. We lose the ability to act calmly, deliberately, and independently. Stoicism teaches that reason is an expression of strength. It reflects a mind that cannot be influenced by outside forces, and will never use outside forces to justify any action or decision. Reason begins in taking responsibility for the condition of our own lives.

If anything, a university should value knowledge, and be about encouraging us to do so. As such, what are we to make of all the ignorance that comes with inclusion policies and politics on college campuses? In fact, what are we to make of the open hostility to knowledge, and thus all the cruelty that come with these policies and politics. What kind of indictment does this represent for higher education? To value knowledge is to believe that it saves us from the ravages of ignorance. Through knowledge we should become less afraid of the world by becoming less afraid of ourselves. Therefore through knowledge we should become less cruel, less violent, less under the control of our instincts, impulses, and desires. This, again, is what distinguishes learning from schooling. Learning transforms us by enlarging us. It gives us dominion over the condition of our lives. This is why learning matters.

CHAPTER 2

NOTES ON AN INCLUSION AFFAIR

I ncidents involving violation of diversity and inclusion norms are now happening on many US university campuses. They usually begin with the surfacing of a video that captures a student, a teacher, or an administrator saying or doing something that is commonly judged to be offensive, derogatory, and hurtful. The chancellor will immediately release a statement condemning those involved and claiming that such behavior has no place at the school. Protests and marches will then follow, with students demanding university administrators respond to a list of demands so as to make the campus safe and inclusive for minority students. There will also be forums and town hall meetings across the campus organized by administrators where minority students will air grievances, frustrations, and struggles.

Such an incident recently happened at Syracuse University. How the university handled the incident demonstrates how the university's diversity and inclusion policy works to diminish communication, and ultimately suppress diversity. Indeed, everything about how the university handled the incident is both disturbing and chilling, especially when seen from the perspective that Syracuse University is supposed to be an institution of higher learning.

The incident involved private videos of satirical sketches done off campus by members of an engineering fraternity, Theta Tau. The videos were posted on a private Facebook group for members of the fraternity, but someone made a recording of a fraternity member's computer screen and sent the videos to the student newspaper and university officials. Chancellor Kent Syverud immediately put out a statement condemning the videos.

Dear Students, Faculty and Staff:

Earlier today, Syracuse University learned of extremely troubling and disturbing conduct at one of our professional fraternity chapters.

Videos showing this offensive behavior have surfaced online. They include words and behaviors that are extremely racist, anti-semitic, homophobic, sexist, and hostile to people with disabilities. I am appalled and shaken by this and deeply concerned for all members of our community.

The conduct is deeply harmful and contrary to the values and community standards we expect of our students. There is absolutely no place at Syracuse University for behavior or language that degrades any individual or group's race, ethnicity, sexuality, gender identity, disability or religious beliefs.

Upon confirming the fraternity involvement, the University's Office of Student Rights and Responsibilities immediately suspended the fraternity, effectively halting all activities. At this time, all evidence has been turned over to the Department of Public Safety, which has launched a formal investigation to identify individuals involved and to take additional legal and disciplinary action.

Syracuse University is committed to fostering a community where all our students feel welcome and are treated with dignity and respect. This behavior is unacceptable and contradicts our moral standards.

What happened at this fraternity serves as a reminder that violations of codes of honor, behavior and values will be met with swift and appropriate consequences.

The University will communicate further on this matter later today, including about other steps and resources we will make available to our community.

Sincerely,
Chancellor Kent Syverud

The Department of Public Safety Chief Bobby Maldonado quickly announced that complaints had been filed against 18 students involved in the videos. The students were accused of violating Syracuse University's Code of Student Conduct. Chief Maldonado and other university administrators publicly promised that the investigation will be "pursued with vigor" and punitive actions (either suspension or expulsion) will be taken against those found guilty. ("*What happened at Theta Tau serves as a reminder that violations of codes of honor, behavior and values will be met with swift and appropriate consequences.*") University administrators also publicly promised an expedited judicial hearing process so that graduation saves no offending student from the fraternity from punishment. In fact, all of the students charged with violating the university's code of conduct were banned from graduation proceedings even before being found guilty of anything. The accused students were also immediately removed from all classes for "safety concerns," and the fraternity was expelled from campus before being found guilty of anything.

There were also calls from the university community for the accused students to be immediately expelled before, again, being found guilty of anything. In many letters to the editor, professors and students said things like, "Our campus has been affronted with a video that represents a deep-seated culture of racism, misogyny, homophobia and ableism of which our university is a part. Students are justifiably outraged." Many academic departments at Syracuse University also released statements expressing solidarity with those students who were supposedly "harmed" by the videos and now felt increasingly "unsafe" on campus.

We, the undersigned, who are faculty in the School of Education, publicly affirm our commitment to all marginalized and oppressed students on campus. The recent video is just one more indication and reminder of the interconnected ways that white supremacy is advanced at Syracuse University and in our communities through racist, homophobic, transphobic, ableist, sexist and anti-Semitic practices. True freedom can only occur when all forms of violence, hatred and systems of domination are dismantled. We join with our students to call on the administration and our fellow faculty to engage in the crucial work of dismantling settler colonialism, white supremacy, heterosexist patriarchy, ableism, transphobia, homophobia, antisemitism, xenophobia and Islamophobia, in addition to other systems and expressions of domination. These expressions of hate and violence don't start with the fraternity house, but are foundational to the structures and cultures on campus. Any expression of hatred, bias, microaggression and other types of violence means we have failed as educators.

The emphasis on diversity and inclusion and implicit bias training is an insufficient response. A comprehensive approach in every dimension of the university to increase the number of underrepresented and undocumented students on campus, scholarship and fellowship opportunities, . . . graduate and undergraduate research support, access to student group funding and curricular and programming efforts is necessary. As an educational and academic institution, a prominent presence of interdisciplinary academic programs to research and teach on the areas of social justice, violence, discrimination and marginalization is also needed to align the university's mission to the knowledge production that continues the work of dismantling structural violence. All students should expect to be supported and nurtured on campus and challenged to become agents of social change and transformation.

Sincerely,
Faculty, School of Education

⟨∞⟩

In light of the recent exposure of two videos recorded and published by members of Theta Tau fraternity—videos revealing fraternity members' trivialization of sexual assault and the use of slurs against disabled, Jewish, Black, LGBTQ2+, and Latinx communities— the Department of Communication and Rhetorical Studies stands unequivocally with marginalized students who routinely experience violence and discrimination on our campus, too often without community, faculty, and administrative support.

We believe that these videos and the behavior of members of [the fraternity] represent broader systems of racism, anti-Semitism, sexism, homophobia, xenophobia, Islamophobia, and ableism. Organizations like [this fraternity] are created and sustained through ritual – in this case, induction ceremonies for new members. Ritual performances of this kind cultivate the idea that it is acceptable and even humorous to dehumanize those marginalized in our society. They send a message to others that some people do not belong. These ritual performances normalize forms of violent behavior, including sexual assault, stereotyping, discrimination, dehumanization, exclusion, and physical violence against marginalized peoples.

The Chancellor and his administration have already taken the important steps of holding town hall meetings to hear students' grievances and permanently expelling the . . . fraternity. A criminal investigation is ongoing, as is a review of Greek life at the University.

We applaud the University's responses so far. We also believe that additional concrete actions could send a compelling message from the Administration indicating a material commitment to its marginalized and oppressed students. Increasing resources for scholarships for minority and disadvantaged students would make such a clear statement. Calling into question the entire Greek Life system would help to get at how the insular rituals of some student organizations perpetuate discrimination and violence.

Hundreds of student activists have come together to form a movement called RecognizeUs. They are developing a list of concrete actions the University could take to address racism, sexism, homophobia, ableism, anti-immigrant sentiment, and all other forms of oppression. We stand in solidarity with those students, a number of whom we are proud to have as majors in our department. As communication scholars invested in social justice, they know that collectively raising the voices of all students is a powerful way to make social change. We commit to doing what we can to support these students in their efforts.

The videos made by members of the . . . fraternity represent some of the worst enactments of the abuse of marginalized and oppressed students. We are under no illusions that these reprehensible ideas are limited to [this fraternity] or to the Greek Life system. The Department of Communication and Rhetorical Studies is committed to education in and the practice of communication designed to challenge those ideas and to build a diverse, inclusive University community through the process of free and open collective public expression of students' interests and goals.

Signed,
Faculty, Communication and Rhetorical Studies Department

Finally, the Chancellor issued other statements promising a series of actions to address students' concerns, including: a) conducting a top to bottom review of all our Greek life policies, activities and culture, b) requiring all Greek and student organization leaders, members and advisors to participate in implicit bias training and inclusivity training, c) providing mandatory training for all students, new and continuing, about the culture and expectations of our community, d) expanding Residence Life training related to diversity and inclusion and implicit bias training, e) enhancing new student orientation and first-year forum and seminars to address diversity and inclusion, implicit bias, alcohol and drugs, and other related topics, f) facilitating dialogue and soliciting feedback among students, faculty and staff through extended open office hours with the dean and department chairs, college meetings, leadership meetings, department meetings, small group discussions, classroom discussions, and online venues, g) forming diversity councils, reviewing curricular practices and re-examining processes for hiring and promotion, h) promoting training on diversity, inclusion and bias, i) hiring more staff to address diversity and inclusion issues in different support programs, like the LBGT Resource Center, and j) taking other concrete steps to address and improve the student culture and experience of all students in the college, with an emphasis on diversity and inclusion as well as overall student success.

Before the judicial hearings for the accused students began, Gregory L. Germain, a professor of law at Syracuse University's College of Law, who was appointed procedural advisor for the accused students, publicly pleaded with the university to show compassion and forgiveness, sensitivity and understanding, as the students never intended to be offensive. Indeed, what emerged from the investigation is that the students who were charged with all manner of heinous things were actually "doing roasts in an attempt to satirize and criticize racism." Also, the students were from diverse racial, religious, and political backgrounds. In fact, nearly half of the fraternity body was of minority backgrounds. Germain asked the university to consider "community mediation" where the accused students could talk with administrators, faculty, and student representatives from groups maligned by the videos. He also proposed a dialogue forum where all involved could learn something from each other and arrive at a solution that could benefit all. He also encouraged the chancellor to meet personally with the students. The university rejected all of Germain's proposals. There would be no communication, only accusations and condemnations. Germain said the university's only offers to the accused students were suspension or expulsion.

The students involved in the videos were eventually found guilty of all charges and received suspensions of up to two years. The suspended students were also to complete a set of diversity and inclusion-related tasks before returning to campus, including: a) reading three books on inclusion, b) writing a 12-page reflection paper on what it means to be a member of a diverse community, and c) performing 160 hours of community service. The students were found guilty of violating a university policy prohibiting "destructive behavior." The judicial board adjudicating the hearing (comprised of only staff and administrators) said the satirical skits threatened the mental health, physical health, and safety of people who sought out and viewed the videos of the event. The university also said that the students involved in the videos violated Syracuse University's policies prohibiting "harassment," which was defined by the university as expression "beyond the bounds of protected speech, directed at a specific individual (s), easily construed as "fighting words," or likely to cause an immediate breach of the peace." Reacting to the ruling, Germain said that "the students were convicted of harassment and threatening people's mental health for performing a roast that offended no one in the room because they all knew it was a joke. Unless corrected, that determination [ruling] will result in a scarlet letter on their official academic records, making it very difficult for the students to transfer to another school to continue their education, or to obtain the benefits that they are paying dearly for."

The university said in a statement issued by Robert Hradsky, Dean of Students, that it treated the "investigation and student conduct process fairly and expeditiously [and] it is now time for our community to focus on the important work of advancing a more inclusive campus community." There was no mention of whether the students were treated sensitively and compassionately. In another statement, the university promised to move quickly to establish an Office of Inclusive Excellence in the College of Engineering and Computer Science, and explore the possibility of establishing other such offices in other schools and colleges. New hires were also made to the university's Office of Equal Opportunity, Inclusion, and Resolution Services. The university also announced the hiring of a director for the university's new Center for Teaching and

Learning Excellence that would, among other things, attend to diversity and equity, and inclusion of marginalized populations.

The decision by the university to expel the fraternity and suspend the students involved in the videos was met with broad support across campus. In letters to the editor, students applauded the university for "attempting to create a safer and more inclusive environment for the entire student body." Indeed, according to Syracuse University's official mission statement, the university strives to foster "a richly diverse and inclusive community." Chancellor Syverud also promised the campus community in the wake of the controversy that Syracuse University would continue to strive to be an "inclusive, student-focused research university."

Unpacking the Reaction

The reaction by university administrators, faculty, and students assumes that the problem was with what the video captures the students saying and doing. Uttering supposedly offensive words supposedly has no place on a college campus that aims to provide "a safe and secure learning environment." Thus those who represent such words and behaviors presumably need to be dealt with harshly and punitively. In my view, however, what is really troubling is how university administrators and faculty are responding to these kinds of diversity incidents in ways that corrupt the mission of higher education, which is to promote the value of knowledge and encourage us to be vulnerable to knowledge. We can identify twelve concerns that are troubling from a pedagogical and theoretical standpoint.

#1 Ignorance Matters

No university administrator or faculty member has any right to adopt a hostile and vengeful stance against any student or group of students. A college campus is a place of both ignorance and knowledge. If there were no ignorance, there would be no need for schools. It is the reality of ignorance that legitimizes learning and the quest for knowledge. Put differently, if there is no place for ignorance on a college campus, then where is a person of ignorance to go to find knowledge? Thus, how can schools claim to be places of learning, and then in the face of ignorance (or supposed ignorance) immediately call in the police and demand that those who are supposedly ignorant be removed (either suspended or expelled) and deprived of knowledge, and thereby the ability to learn and become anew? Where then is ignorance to go to find enlightenment? Indeed, what is the irony, really tragedy, in this recent case is that the Chancellor of Syracuse University, as the controversy was unfolding, was highlighting the fact that the university was conducting interviews with finalists "for a founding director of the Center for Teaching and Learning Excellence. . . . The center will serve as a resource to help our faculty enhance their pedagogical skills, inclusive of cultural competencies." However, what is the value of any center for teaching and learning for an institution of learning that wants nothing to do with ignorance?

#2 Pedagogy Matters

Teaching is about taking sides on how we engage ignorance. To teach is to assume that ignorance is best engaged peacefully and dialogically rather than violently and confrontationally. Indeed, teaching is about assuming that there is no place for any kind of violence when engaging ignorance. Ideally, teaching is about coming to terms with the origins and implications of our own ignorance. In other words, teaching is a gentle activity. As teachers, the most we can do is invite, encourage, and seduce. We have no business insidiously imposing our beliefs, values, and positions on our students. As such, no university administrator or faculty member should ever say that certain words are inherently offensive, especially before knowing the context in which those words occurred, and what was intended by those using those words. As teachers, our first responsibility is to model for our students a dialogic stance, which means, among many other things, refraining from judging and condemning others before we hear all sides. As Steve Leder, author of *More Beautiful Than Before: How Suffering Transforms Us*, reminds us, injecting "some doubt into our self-righteousness" is necessary for harmony. "Only doubt enables us to consider, *Maybe it's me. Maybe she is right. Maybe he does have a point. Maybe I was unkind. Maybe I was too severe, insecure, self-righteous, proud, or aggressive. Maybe I was wrong.*" In short, in a dialogic stance there is no place for self righteousness as we have no ability to know everything. There is always more to know, more to understand. When these incidents occur on a college campus, a Chancellor would be better served by saying something like, "I understand how these videos appear disturbing. However, before I can comment further I need to meet with the students involved and get a better understanding of what the videos are capturing. This is consistent with our policy at this university to first listen and understand before we judge and denounce. I therefore ask for patience as this process unfolds." Behind this kind of statement is the belief that dignity matters, that all students at any university should be treated with dignity, and that dignity begins with giving persons the benefit of the doubt. In the words of Donna Hicks (2018), author of *Leading With Dignity: How to Create a Culture that Brings out the Best in People*, giving others the benefit of the doubt means treating "people as if they are trustworthy," starting from "the premise that others have good motives and are acting with integrity" (p. 17). Thus, for the Chancellor and faculty of Syracuse University to take the view that the members of Theta Tau were undeserving of any kind of dignity, and to model this view in an educational setting, should be most disturbing to any person who professes to care about teaching and the well-being of students.

#3 Expectations Matter

The university issued another statement after the students were found guilty saying that it "stands by the actions it took to protect the well-being of the campus community and to maintain a respectful and safe learning environment." However, no university should ever promise students a safe and secure campus, that is, a campus that is devoid of all the things that come with ignorance and dealing with ignorance. The mission of a university is to engage ignorance peacefully and dialogically. Ignorance will always be rampant on college campuses, just like how sickness is rampant in hospitals. Yet there is nothing pleasant about dealing with ignorance, just like how there is nothing pleasant about dealing with sickness. Nor are there any pedagogical strategies that come with guarantees. Most often we will fail in our mission as teachers. Ignorance will often prevail, even in the face of our best and most strenuous efforts. The tragic demise of every prophet reminds us of this reality. The best we can do as teachers is our best. Ignorance is also about all the things that come with ignorance—the apathy, the arrogance, the lack of curiosity, the lack of effort, the lack of patience, the lack of self discipline. Nothing about dealing with ignorance is easy or certain. Just as much as no hospital administrator can promise patients a hospital that is safe from disease, no university administrator should promise students a campus that is safe from ignorance. Schools succeed when our students learn to engage ignorance peacefully and dialogically. A college education should be profoundly unsettling, beyond the bounds of what any person or group considers civil and decent. No campus can be a refuge from ignorance and still hold true to its primary mission, which is to help students nurture the skills and temperament to deal with ignorance peacefully and dialogically.

Learning involves challenging everything we value, believe, and fear, thereby disrupting how we perceive, experience, and make sense of things. Simply put, learning succeeds by being unsettling, by pushing us to do things that are difficult and even disturbing. That learning involves challenging what we believe and value means that learning involves challenging our notions of decency and civility. Any effort to block this kind of reckoning impedes learning by insidiously undermining the honesty, intensity, and ferocity that is necessary to disrupt our notions of decency and civility. Indeed, to demand, either explicitly or implicitly, that class discussions and readings conform to a certain sensibility is to miss the fact that learning is obligated to disrupt everything, especially what we hold to be sacred. Nothing can be off limits in learning, and invoking race, gender, disability, religion, or sexual orientation to make believe otherwise only stops learning from succeeding. As Henry A. Giroux, Professor of English and Cultural Studies at McMaster University, notes, "Creating safe spaces runs counter to the notion that learning should be unsettling, that students should challenge common sense assumptions and be willing to confront disturbing realities despite discomfort." Indeed, "confronting the intolerable should be challenging and upsetting." It should be "the conditions that produce violence that should upset us ethically and prompt us to act responsibly, rather than to capitulate to a privatized emotional response that substitutes a therapeutic language for a political and worldly one." For Wendy Brown, Professor of Political Science at University of California, Berkeley, "the domain of free public speech is not one of emotional safety or reassurance" and is "not what the public sphere and political speech promise." Instead, a university education should "call you to think, question, doubt" and "incite you to question everything you assume, think you know or care about." Similarly, Van Jones believes that the rise of language politics on college campuses undermines a rigorous liberal democracy. Speaking at the University of Chicago, Jones said that the notion held by students that "I need to be safe ideologically, I need to be safe emotionally, I just need to feel good all the time. . .

and if someone else says something that I don't like that is a problem for everyone else, including the administration," is a "terrible idea" because it undermines the mission of a university education. "I don't want you to be safe ideologically. I don't want you to be safe emotionally. I want you to be strong. That's different. I'm not going to pave the jungle for you. Put on some boots and learn how to deal with adversity. I'm not going to take the weights out of the gym. That's the whole point of the gym. This is the gym [university]. You can't live on a campus where people say stuff that you don't like." Moreover, "You are creating a kind of liberalism that . . . is not just useless, but obnoxious and dangerous. I want you to be offended every single day on this campus. I want you to be deeply aggrieved and offended and upset, and then to learn how to speak back. Because that is what we need from you." In sum, a college education should be profoundly unsettling, beyond the bounds of what any person or group considers civil and decent. After all, as Simon Critchley, Hans Jonas Professor of Philosophy at the New School for Social Research in New York, observes, "Nothing is more common in the history of philosophy than the accusation of impiety."

#4 Restorative Justice Matters

It is disheartening to hear university administrators and faculty call for punitive measures for students accused of engaging in supposedly offensive behavior. After all, even animal trainers know well that pain has no place in the training of animals. Pain, regardless of what form it takes, makes us less human, corroding the humanity of those who are subject to it and those who inflict it. Indeed, psychology departments know a lot about the ravages of pain (Haney, 2009). It should have no place in any institution of higher learning. Why then do university administrators, faculty, and students have no qualms about demanding punitive measures for those students accused of engaging in supposedly offensive behavior? How does the university's modeling of punitive measures enable the healing and repairing of ignorance? Where are the demands and statements from academic departments when these incidents arise for restorative justice? Instead of police investigations and expedited hearings to decide what students will be suspended or expelled, why are there no calls and recommendations for peace and reconciliation committees to deal with these kinds of incidents? How did mercy and forgiveness come to have no prominent place in a higher learning setting, and what becomes the value of any education that never highlights these notions?

#5 Communication Matters

Where is communication theory in how university administrators, faculty, and students are responding to these incidents involving supposedly offensive words and behaviors? Chancellor Syverud said that the videos "include words and behaviors that are extremely racist, anti-semitic, homophobic, sexist, and hostile to people with disabilities." However, this description is subjective rather than objective, evaluative rather than descriptive. In short, this description is contrary to a fundamental tenet in communication theory, which is that meaning resides in people rather than in words. So before I can condemn your words, I need to know first what you meant, as in *What exactly did you mean? What was your intent? Was there malice?* As Virginia P. Richmond and James C. McCroskey (2009) note, "The idea that meanings are in words is perhaps the most common misconception about communication. . . . No word has any meaning apart from the person using it. No two people share precisely the same meaning for all words. *Meaning are in people, not words.* Therefore, we must realize that what we say to others . . . might not convey the meaning we intend" (p. 17). For Sheila Steinberg (2006), author of *Introduction To Communication*, "words are arbitrary signs that members of a culture agree to use to represent the things they sense and experience. It is because meaning does not reside in words that different cultures can also agree that *hond, chien, injha, mpya,* and *dog* can be used to talk about the same animal" (p. 49). Being communicatively competent is about always attending to four questions: (1) *What is intended?* That is, what meaning is the person seeking to convey? This question assumes that what a person is intending to mean can be different from what the person seems to be meaning. (2) *What is interpreted?* That is, what meaning is being derived from our words and actions? This question assumes that we have no reliable control over how others interpret our words and actions. (3) *What is distorted?* That is, because human beings are of different experiences, different perspectives, different resources, different environments, our words and actions are vulnerable to different interpretations and distortions. Finally, (4) *What is impacted?* That is, how is the medium in any communication impacting what meaning is intended and what meaning is interpreted? This question assumes that every medium impacts communication differently. Common expressions like, "Yes, I know what you said, but what exactly do you mean?" and "I know what I said, but that is not what I meant" also remind us that meaning often exceeds language and symbols. Many different things shape and influence what things mean to different people. In order to understand what I mean, you have to pay attention to many different things. In fact, determining what any person means is difficult and complex as our experiences and worldviews can be fundamentally different. There is simply no reliable way to know what a person means. As Lee Thayer explains, "Systems of every size are complex—including conversations. You cannot say something and expect it will be understood as you intended. It lands on the complex minds of other people. They will interpret what you say as they intend—and as is necessary for them." Thus, "In human communication there will always be collateral damage. There will be residual and accompanying effects you may not have intended."

Communication requires restraint, generosity, and grace. We should give others the benefit of the doubt and be generous in our interpretations of things. We should even be ready to be wrong. As Martha Nussbaum, Ernst Feund Distinguished Service Professor of Law and Ethics at the University of Chicago, writes in *Cultivating Humanity: A Classical Defense of Reform in Liberal Education,* "The first step of understanding the point of view of the other is essential to any responsible act of judgment, since we do not know what we are judging until we see the meaning of an action as the person intends it, the meaning of speech as it expresses something of importance in the context of that person's history and social world."

Another fundamental tenet in communication theory is that meaning is bound up with context. As Gregory Bateson notes, "without context there is no communication." In order to understand what your words might mean I need to understand the context situating your words. In short, words mean nothing outside of context. As regards communication, contexts exceed words in terms of what is truly important. Without contexts, words are meaningless. Meaning is created, guided, and shaped by contexts. Consequently, no word is inherently racist or sexist. What words mean must always be understood within a context. Yet knowing what context is shaping the meaning of any word (or set of words) is all but impossible to know reliably as there are many forces (e.g., racial, cultural, historical, political) that shape the context that in turn shape the meaning of words. Thus, any position that begins on the premise that certain words are inherently offensive reflects no rigorous understanding of communication theory. So again, no Chancellor or university administrator is in any position to say that certain words (or behaviors) are inherently offensive, defamatory, and hurtful. However, much more troubling is when communication departments issue statements saying that "that these videos and the behavior of members of [the fraternity] represent broader systems of racism, anti-Semitism, sexism, homophobia, xenophobia,

Islamophobia, and ableism," especially when never knowing—or even seeking to know—what were the accused students' intent or the context situating and framing the words and behaviors. Upon being forced to resign in the face of yet another of these campus incidents, Tim Wolfe, President of University of Missouri, said something in his final remarks that remains relevant, "Change comes from listening, learning, caring, and conversation. . . . We have to respect each other enough to stop yelling at each other and start listening."

#6 Democracy Matters

When dealing with these kinds of incidents, university administrators and faculty tend to undermine teaching as a democratic practice. To engage teaching dialogically is to promote teaching as a democratic practice that ultimately aims to cultivate a democratic consciousness. We are all different, all of different experiences, different resources, different environments, different influences, different circumstances, and thus all of different rationalities, sensibilities, modalities, capacities, and spiritualities. There is no truth or reality that is ever outside of our diversity. However, because of our diversity, any truth can mean different things to each of us. So the fact that you may be outraged by hearing certain words in no way means that the rest of us, even those of us of the same race, gender, or grouping, are equally outraged, or should be equally outraged. It also means that how you choose to engage a problem can be different from how I choose to do so. Promoting teaching as a democratic practice is about recognizing and reckoning with our diversity. We have to be always vulnerable to perspectives that are different and even contrary to our own. In all things, our goal as teachers should be to model a democratic consciousness for our students. This means, among many other things, choosing to listen rather than condemn. Democracy begins in communication, as in us always allowing for the possibility of a different truth, a different perspective, a different meaning, a different reality.

Communication is the womb of possibility. In order for diversity to flourish, democracy must flourish, and in turn communication must flourish. Thus to watch university administrators and faculty put out statements that reflect no understanding of this sacred relationship between democracy, diversity, and communication is disturbing on many different levels. For what is the value of any education that fails to teach us about the most fundamental of things, especially those things that can help us become better versions of ourselves?

#7 Perspectives Matter

Diversity matters because perspectives matter. If anything, diversity is about our different experiences, different circumstances, different struggles, different influences, and different resources making for different perspectives. In valuing your perspective, I am valuing all these different things that make for your different perspective. Valuing different perspectives is also about recognizing and acknowledging the limits of our own perspectives. As much as every person has a different perspective, every perspective has limits and blind spots. No human being is capable of understanding anything completely and absolutely. Learning is about recognizing the limits of our perspectives, which means that learning is about cultivating humility and vulnerability. So again, what is disturbing about the handling of the incident at Syracuse University is the unwillingness of administrators and faculty to learn the perspectives of the accused students before issuing statements of condemnation.

#8 Compassion Matters

Besides the cruel punishment that Syracuse University inflicted on the members of the fraternity involved in the skits, the university also attached scarlett letters to their transcripts, ensuring that this incident permanently scars them. In court filings, the university also sought the right to publicly name all the students involved in the incident. The university's counsel argued that "the public has a substantial interest in the transparency of legal proceedings" and that the students' "desire to limit their association with [the] videos that may cause them embarrassment does not outweigh that interest." Transparency is no doubt important, but how would publicly naming the students promote any kind of learning or doing anything positive for the students? Put differently, how did the university come to have no qualms about further embarrassing, humiliating, and harming its own students? What did the university seek to gain from being openly and publicly hostile to its own students? In short, what to make of all this cruelty from an institution of higher learning? Why would any university want to inflict this kind of permanent and debilitative punishment on students for a nonviolent offense? In statement after statement, Syracuse University said that the student conduct process was handled "fairly and professionally." But in any school setting, this is the wrong standard. The students should be entitled to be treated generously and compassionately. That is, the students should be entitled to be treated in ways that are taught in many courses across the university about mercy, tenderness, and forgiveness. How could any university be of a view that is so contrary to so many important teachings, and how could so many faculty be supportive of this view and the actions the university took against the students? Indeed, most striking about all the statements put out by different academic departments, including the School of Education, is the lack of any concern for the well-being of the accused students. How do certain students become unredeemable, and deserving of scorn and contempt from those responsible for teaching them?

#9 Rigor Matters
As a result of the Theta Tau incident, Syracuse University will now require all students to take a newly developed course that promotes

the values of diversity and inclusion. But this is indoctrination passing as education. Learning demands rigor, meaning that learning assumes that nothing is sacred and thus off limits. In other words, learning is about leaving nothing unexplored and unexamined. It is about laying everything bare, and in the process helping us to recognize the relation between human things (like fears, values, and beliefs) and social and material things (like ideologies, epistemologies, and technologies). To interrogate inclusion is to recognize that this notion is silly. Other than persons who support harming and committing fraud on others, who possesses the moral and cultural authority at Syracuse University to dictate what and who should be included, accommodated, and celebrated. How can this moral and cultural authority be fairly determined and instituted in ways that protect and respect the differences of minority groups and perspectives? Case in point, soon after expelling the Theta Tau fraternity from campus, Syracuse University banned all consensual personal relationships between undergraduates and faculty, that is, between one group of adults and another group of adults. Graduate students and staff are exempt from the ban. In a statement to the university community, Michele G. Wheatly, Provost, said "The safety and well-being of our students is always our top priority, and as a university we are legally required and steadfastly committed to providing a learning, living and working environment that is free from discrimination or harassment. The policy changes represent an important step to ensuring a safe, welcoming and empowering learning environment that supports students' success in the classroom and in their overall University experience." But the Provost never shared with the university community how this ban was conceptually different to other laws and regulations from the past prohibiting other kinds of consensual personal relationships between adults, such as those between adults of different races and those of the same sexual orientation. Neither did the Provost and the many faculty who vigorously pushed for the new policy share with the university community how they arrived at the conclusion that certain adults lacked the emotional and intellectual maturity to navigate certain kinds of relationships.

This new ban was proposed by a group of women faculty at the university, often referred to as the Feminists High Council. However, what of the other feminists at Syracuse University who find the banning of any consensual personal relationship between adults on a college campus to be deeply offensive to women? Case in point, in an essay titled *Hands Off Consensual Sex*, Kal Alston (1998), a Professor of cultural foundations at Syracuse University in the School of Education, claims that such bans assume and perpetuate the notion that certain adult women lack the emotional and intellectual maturity to navigate certain kinds of relationships. After all, claims Alston, "If the student perceives the relationship as consensual, who is going to make the determination that the relationship is asymmetrical and thus abusive? Do we really want to make a rule whose fair enforcement would mean the surveillance, scrutiny, and outside interpretation of our relations and affective displays with students?" (p. 33). Thus, "I do not want to assume a priori that a woman as woman or a student should be stripped of her or his ability to make choices, to participate in adult relations, or to give consent. We cannot know from the outside what the power distribution is in any given relationship simply by knowing the genders and occupations of the participants. Each relationship has a complex set of power relations based on personality, experience, level of commitment, affective investment, mobility, and other factors" (p. 33). Indeed, most student-professor relationships are initiated by the student, many of these relationships tend to be meaningful and long-term, and issues related to age, race/ethnicity, and sexuality tend to bring greater challenges than student/professor status differences for those involved in such relationships (Bellas & Gossett, 2001; Skeen & Nielsen, 1983). The reality is that these bans on consensual personal relationships between adults "give administrators vast new powers over faculty" and make faculty vulnerable to all kinds of mischief and persecution from disgruntled colleagues. As Neil McArthur (2017) explains,

> Bans on consensual relationships by definition create a crime for which there is no victim and no complainant with first-hand knowledge of the situation. There is thus only one way for administrators to find out about a faculty-student relationship: from third parties, either through gossip of through direct accusations. Of all the insidious effects of relationship bans, the encouragement they give to third-party accusations must surely be the most toxic. They give people a potent tool to use against disliked colleagues, either to intimidate them or to have them dismissed—or, through baseless accusations, merely to make their lives difficult. (p. 132)

In short, upon what basis should Kal Alston's perspective be excluded? Put differently, how did Syracuse University come to have the moral and cultural authority to ban a 36 year old woman (an undergraduate) from engaging in a consensual personal relationship that another 22 year woman (a graduate student) is permitted to have? Again, how, and by what means, did such a relationship end up in the realm of exclusion, and how does Syracuse University come to have the moral authority to deprive any person of such a fundamental human right and freedom, that is, to engage in a consensual relationship with another adult of our own choosing?

#10 Faculty Matters

At foundation of the college experience is the relationship between teachers and students. But this relationship is increasingly being undermined by the rise of university administrators. In fact, the ranks of university administrators have been exploding, and at the expense (both pedagogically and financially) of both faculty and students. According to a recent report based on federal data, the number of executive, administrative and managerial employees on university campuses across the US increased by a collective 15 percent between 2007 and 2014 (Hechinger Report, 2016). Moreover, the "ranks of administrators have expanded far faster than the numbers of students and faculty," and at "many four-year institutions, spending on administration has increased faster than spending on instruction." We are to assume that all of these administrative positions are necessary, when in fact nothing could be further from the truth. According to Benjamin Ginsberg (2011), author of *The Fall of the Faculty: The Rise of the All-Administrative University and Why it Matters*, university administrators use inclusion and diversity incidents to expand their ranks and gain more control over faculty and students. This, in fact, is exactly what transpired at Syracuse University after the Theta Tau incident. Although the university had the backing of faculty and students, all the key players involved in prosecuting, adjudicating, and punishing the Theta Tau students were administrators. The university also moved quickly to create and fill many new administrative positions. Yet this ever-expanding administrative power and swelling of administrative ranks, including now the power to control and monitor the personal relationships between faculty and students, would be impossible without the complicity of faculty. All of which now makes for this question, why is faculty so willing to secede power to university administrators, and in doing so undermine the important relationship between teacher and student that is at the foundation of the college experience? The reality is that the Theta Tau incident should have involved no administrators as no kind of crime (meaning no physical harm or fraud) was committed by the students. It merely required a lot of listening, something which is actually taught in many classes at Syracuse University.

#11 Ideology Matters

In a final statement, Syracuse University said that the "Theta Tau fraternity videos presented a situation where the rights of one group to speak freely collide with the rights of others to have a safe and welcoming learning environment." This is false. The fraternity was merely satirizing racism in an off campus building. It was in no way seeking "to speak freely" or even recklessly. The skits were only meant for those who knew the context. Still, the statement goes on to say that,

> The university recognizes that a healthy and rigorous learning environment must allow for a diverse array of ideas, even those that may be viewed by a majority as provocative, or potentially incendiary. The university's speech policies are designed to balance free expression with the university's obligation to maintain an educational environment that is devoid of discrimination or harassment. The university expects members of its campus community to adhere to the standards and values set forth in university policies. The university allows and empowers all students to freely express themselves within these important parameters.

But what exactly does this mean, especially when the university is the final decider of what distinguishes provocative speech from offensive speech? What are Syracuse University's students to learn about democracy when the university possesses all the power to determine what speech is offensive rather than merely provocative, and also to solely determine the fate of those who are unable to reliably do so? For Syracuse University, the controversy is about Syracuse University's role in determining what kind of speech is permissible on a college campus (never mind that the incident occurred off campus). Supposedly, for the sake of learning, certain kinds of speech need to be suppressed. Order must come first, and it is supposedly the responsibility of the university—with a costly and ever-expanding bureaucracy—to produce and maintain it.

Syracuse University is assuming that the world is of an inherent conflict between positive and negative forces, such as life versus death, order versus chaos, knowledge versus ignorance, communication versus confusion, meaning versus ambiguity, and so forth. In this way, Syracuse University is assuming that without the imposition of order, such as instituting codes of conduct to force students to act civilly, chaos will ensue, bringing harm to members of minority peoples and undercutting "a safe and welcoming learning environment." It is supposedly "the university's obligation to maintain an educational environment that is devoid of discrimination or harassment." So without the university playing this vital policing role, which again means having a vast and costly bureaucracy to do so effectively, all kinds of bad things will supposedly occur. But this supposed conflict between positive and negative forces is of our own making. Nothing but a creation of our worldview. It is ideology, pure and simple. Moreover, the imposition of order impedes learning. Syracuse University is mistaking schooling for learning. Schools institutionalize us rather than emancipate us. It is why too many schools have no capacity to teach us anything important. It is also why too many students learn barely anything important in school. Learning can only come from within us. We must first be ready and willing to learn before any teacher can teach us anything. That we are ready and willing to learn means that we are ready and willing to struggle with everything we believe and value. It also means that we are ready and willing to die, metaphorically that is. The order that schools impose impedes learning by saving us from the hardwork that learning demands, beginning with taking responsibility for the condition of our lives. Our redemption can only come from our own doing. This involves engaging directly, honestly, and compassionately those who are of modes of being that conflict with our own, trying to come to terms with the origins and implications of our differences, and recognizing that nothing about any of this is easy. Moreover, in demanding institutional solutions to language issues and conflicts, colleges move these issues and conflicts from the individual realm to the institutional realm, in the process undermining individual agency and autonomy. That is, besides undermining human diversity, colleges, in relying on institutional solutions to various kinds of issues and tensions between students, undercut individual initiative and responsibility. As Neil Postman (1979) explains in *Teaching as a Conserving Activity*,

> Once an institution takes on a problem, to some extent individuals are released from the obligation to solve it themselves. It is true enough that much of the pain and inconvenience of modern life are systemic in their origin and cannot be eliminated without social and or political action. . . . But it is not true that every difficulty, every inadequacy, every failing, is entirely social in origin and beyond the range of personal control. Although the liberal point of view does not easily admit it, each person has the capability to take responsibility for some part of his or her life, and of altering that which is painful or destructive. (p. 118)

Indeed, taking on this kind of responsibility for the condition of our lives is vital for human flourishing.

#12 Students Matter

Finally, university administrators and faculty handle these incidents in ways that undermine the primary mission of higher education, which is to encourage our students to make the world better by becoming better versions of themselves. We are all susceptible to all kinds of primal instincts and impulses. However, through learning, meaning through rigorous reflection and self examination, we acquire the capacity to control these instincts and impulses. So through learning we should become less arrogant, less violent, less impatient, less indifferent. We should become so because mind and heart are bound up with each other. Expanding our minds demands enlarging our hearts. Mumford and Sons capture this reality well in the song *Awake My Soul*, "If you lend me your eyes I can change what you see, but first your soul must remain perfectly free." The point being that our students have to deal with a world that is increasingly plural and multicultural, and also one that is increasingly fraught with peril. Our students have to become better global citizens for this world to flourish. This means being able to handle conflict and tension dialogically and democratically rather than confrontationally and autocratically. Thus every incident on a campus, regardless of however wrenching and disturbing, should be an exercise in becoming so.

Conclusion

The corporatization and defunding of higher education should concern us all. But these are by no means the most serious threats to higher education, or what passes for higher education. How did higher education become hostile to ignorance? How did ignorance become a crime on a college campus? Also, how did higher education come to mistake tyranny for diversity? For to demand that all of us find offensive what another finds to be offensive is tyranny rather than diversity. This requires, after all, downplaying our diversity, as in my sensibility being different to yours, my rationality being different to yours, my spirituality being different to yours, my modality being different to yours, and so forth. How did places of higher learning become hostile to diversity? Indeed, how did such places come to value conformity over diversity?

All perspectives are by no means morally, politically, and epistemologically equal. However, diversity is about allowing for the possibility of a different truth, a different reality, a different interpretation, a different perspective. It is about nurturing and affirming possibility. This is how diversity resides in communication. Rather than in us, diversity resides between us. It demands grace, generosity, and restraint in order to flourish. So when communication collapses, diversity collapses. This is why communication is so foundational to the human experience. It makes democracy possible, and in doing so makes diversity possible.

Colleges have long been integral in maintaining the status quo. We need only remember the sordid role that colleges played in preserving slavery and Jim Crow. But then there are the many insidious ways that colleges maintain the status quo. There are the institutional and epistemological practices that make the pursuit of bold new questions extremely difficult. As Thomas Kuhn observed long ago, science wants nothing to do with diversity.

The point being that the criminalizing of ignorance on college campuses reflects much larger concerns about higher education. Before colleges can be corporatized, colleges must be susceptible to being corporatized. The proposition of corporatization has to be plausible to colleges. In my view, this plausibility begins in the recognition that colleges are first and foremost institutions, and the primary directive of an institution is to achieve and preserve order by suppressing and eliminating chaos. Colleges assume that without order, learning is impossible. Order supposedly makes learning possible. Order, of course, means conformity and hierarchy, such as demanding that students obediently conform to arbitrary codes of conduct or face suspension and expulsion. In this way, colleges are in no way different to any other kind corporation in terms of viewing chaos (or what is perceived to be chaos) as a threat to all that is good and valuable. The imposition of order is supposedly necessary for our safety. Thus ending the criminalizing of ignorance on colleges campuses is going to involve reimagining and reconfiguring everything that constitutes higher education.

CHAPTER 3

PROBLEMS WITH LANGUAGE POLITICS

A key element in any diversity and inclusion policy is the belief that certain kinds of language inherently have the power to hurt and harm, and thus need to be institutionally suppressed for the sake of achieving diversity and inclusion. This belief has given rise to what is now commonly referred to as *language politics*—different kinds of initiatives to suppress certain kinds of language because they are supposedly inherently offensive and cause existential and psychological harm. The following movements are examples of language politics:

A. Heresy and blasphemy laws. Laws "limiting the freedom of speech and expression relating to blasphemy, or irreverence toward holy personages, religious artifacts, customs, or beliefs."

B. Speech codes. Rules and regulations that aim to stop the "infliction of psychological and/or emotional harm upon any member of the University community through any means, including but not limited to email, social media, and other technological forms of communication."

C. Trigger warnings. Notices used to warn readers or listeners about any contents (spoken or written) that could potentially be upsetting or traumatizing.

D. Microaggressions. Commonly defined as "everyday verbal, nonverbal, and environmental slights, snubs, or insults, whether intentional or unintentional, which communicate hostile, derogatory, or negative messages to target persons based solely upon their marginalized group membership."

E. University language covenants. Colleges requiring—for the supposed sake of promoting civility, collegiality, and diversity— new students to sign contracts agreeing to abide by certain speech codes.

F. Hate speech laws. Generally defined as "publications which express profound disrespect, hatred, and vilification for members of minority groups." United Kingdom, Germany, France, Denmark, Australia, and Canada all have laws criminalizing hate speech.

In the *Harm in Hate Speech,* Jeremy Waldron claims that hate speech should be suppressed because it undermines both the security and dignity of members of minority groups. As for security, Walron (2012a) writes, "each person, each member of each group, should be able to go about his or her business, with the assurance that there will be no need to face hostility, violence, discrimination, or exclusion by others" (p. 4). According to Waldron, "This sense of security in the space we inhabit is a public good, and in a good society it is something that we all contribute to and help sustain in an instinctive and almost noticeable way" (p. 4). As regards hate speech undermining the dignity of minority peoples, Waldron claims that a person's dignity "is their social standing, the fundamentals of basic reputation that entitle them to be treated as equals in the ordinary operations of society. Their dignity is something they can rely on—in the best case implicitly and without fuss, as they live their lives, go about their business, and raise their families" (p. 5). According to Waldron, "The publication of hate speech is calculated to undermine this. Its aim is to compromise the dignity of those at whom it is targeted, both in their own eyes and the eyes of other members of society" (p. 5).

Waldron defines hate speech as "the use of words which are deliberately abusive and/or insulting and/or threatening and/or demeaning directed at members of vulnerable minorities, calculated to stir up hatred against them" (pp. 8-9). On the other hand, Waldron has reservations about the phrase "hate speech" and would prefer we focus on "more enduring artifacts of racist expression" that are visible and public. He writes, "The issue is publication and the harm done to individuals and groups through the disfiguring of our social environment by visible, public, and semipermanent announcements to the effect that in the opinion of one group in the community, perhaps the majority, members of another group are not worthy of equal citizenship" (p. 39). Waldron claims that because hate speech causes social harm, it stops us from achieving a "well-ordered society," one where all members respect each other's dignity and enjoy the mutual assurance and safety that they can go about the business of living their lives without any fear of discrimination, humiliation, and sanction. He contends that hate speech is like pornography in this regard, and devotes a few pages revisiting Catharine MacKinnon's case against pornography and how hate speech functions "similarly" for minority groups. Waldron claims that no well-ordered society will allow any minority group to be socially harmed. He also claims that hate speech is different to offensive speech, and the latter should be permissible in a well-ordered society.

Waldron believes that the distinction between hate speech and offensive speech is easy to make. He writes,

> Individual Christians, millions of them, are entitled to protection against defamation, including defamation as Christians. But this does not mean that any pope, saint or doctrine is to be protected, nor does it mean that the reputation of Jesus is to be protected. . . . By the same token, individual Muslims, millions of them, are entitled to protection against defamation, including defamation as Muslims. But that doesn't mean that the prophet Muhammad is to be protected against defamation or the creedal beliefs of the group. The civic duty of the group stands separately from the status of their beliefs, however offensive an attack upon the prophet or even the Koran may seem. (p. 123)

For Waldron, the British Public Order Act captures this distinction best. It stipulates that "a person who uses threatening, abusive or insulting words or behaviour, or displays any written material which is threatening, abusive or insulting, is guilty of an offence if (a) he intends thereby to stir up racial hatred, or (b) having regard to all the circumstances racial hatred is likely to be stirred up thereby." On the other hand, nothing in the statute "shall be read or given effect in a way which prohibits or restricts discussion, criticism or expressions of antipathy, dislike, ridicule, insult or abuse of particular religions or the beliefs or practices of their adherents, or of any other belief system or the beliefs or practices of its adherents, or proselytizing or urging adherents of a different religion or belief system to cease practicing their religion or belief system" (Waldron, 2012b).

But Waldron's distinction between hate speech and offensive speech has no relation to the real world. For most persons who are religiously devout, there is simply no conception of dignity that has nothing to do with religion. For these persons, Waldron's distinction between hate speech and offensive speech will never make any kind of sense, and thus will never be tolerated. This is why Newman (2017) calls Waldron's distinction between hate speech and offensive speech "fanciful." According to Newman, "Hate speech is simply a particularly egregious variety of offensive speech, and whether or when one slips over into the other is a purely subjective determination. The ultimate finding is, of course, made by whoever wields the power of censorship" (p. 690). Peter Jones (2015) also finds Waldron's distinction absurd, "It makes no sense to say that of someone's race that it is false, absurd, pernicious, or oppressive; [but] it makes perfectly good sense to say any of these things of a person's religion" (p. 684). Indeed, there is nothing in Waldron's case against hate speech that has any foundation in anything real. It is merely a cerebral exercise, and Waldron acknowledges as much in the end. Also, Waldron never tells us how harm will be determined in ways that have nothing to do with culture and ideology. Case in point, many African Americans want confederate statues to be removed from public spaces because they supposedly cause harm, just like how Waldron contends. But what of the many other African Americans who want the statues to stay put because they serve as reminders of how far they have come? Why should the latter perspective have no place in a well-ordered society that, to use Waldron's words, "values the dignity of inclusion," and what does such opposition reveal about the validity and even usefulness of social harm as a political concept?

For Waldron, dignity is first and foremost a legal concept. It is given to us by law. Thus in order to protect and guarantee it to all, especially members of minority groups, law is necessary. In this case, hate speech law. Also, protecting and guaranteeing dignity to all requires that these laws be punitively and stringently enforced, such as Waldron supporting the criminalizing of hate speech and the British Public Order Act containing provisions that allow for lengthy prison sentences for offenders. For Waldron, hate speech laws stop others from depriving us of our dignity. In supposedly depriving us of our dignity, hate speech inflicts harm on members of minority groups, just as how pornography supposedly inflicts harm on women. Interestingly, Waldron never invokes any kind of scholarship to show the harm hate speech causes. We are simply to assume that certain kinds of speech causes harm by robbing us of our dignity. However, what becomes the value of this dignity that words can rob us off? What also becomes the value of this dignity that is dependent on laws in order to be safe? What happens when hate speech laws are unenforceable, such as when the courts treat one person's hate speech as merely offensive speech, and thus legally permissible? How then to protect my dignity from what I view as my neighbor's hate speech?

In reality, no person can rob us of our dignity. In the words of Archbishop Desmond Tutu, "No one has the power to strip us of our dignity. How do you think we got through apartheid? Knowing that our dignity was in our hands, and in our hands only, sustained us in those darkest moments" (quoted in Hicks, 2018, p. 4). This truth is also found in Nelson Mandela's book *Long Walk to Freedom*. Martin Luther King, Jr.'s autobiography also captures two instances of what dignity looks like. In the first instance a negotiation went sideways. "That Monday I went home with a heavy heart. I was weighed down by a terrible sense of guilt, remembering that on two or three occasions I had allowed myself to become angry and indignant. I had spoken hastily and resentfully. Yet I knew that this was no way to solve a problem. 'You must not harbor anger,' I admonished myself. 'You must be willing to suffer the anger of the opponent, and yet not return anger. You must not become bitter. No matter how emotional your opponents are, you must be calm.'" Then there was the instance after King's house was firebombed, "While I lay in that quiet front bedroom, I began to think of the viciousness of people who would bomb my home. I could feel the anger rising when I realized that my wife and baby could have been killed. I was once more on the verge of corroding hatred. And once more I caught myself and said: 'You must not allow yourself to become bitter.'" In both instances King is compellingly reminding us that dignity is about refusing to become something that others wish us to become. It is about strength, as in being of the strength to remain true to the best versions of ourselves in the face of evil and torment. As Donna Hicks (2018) nicely explains, "If we mistakenly think our dignity comes only from external sources or from the way others treat us, we are giving up a tremendous amount of internal power—power that gives us resilience, enabling us to ward off assaults and stay firmly grounded in the truth of our worthiness" (p. 5).

No less troubling about Waldron's conception of dignity is the suggestion that peoples and cultures that lack legal codes enforcing dignity are morally deficient. For Waldron, hate speech laws represent moral evolution. It is supposedly what civilized peoples do, devise and enforce laws that protect the dignity of members of minority groups. We are left with the impression that certain peoples and cultures are bereft of conceptions of dignity that are comparable to those that have hate speech laws. But how could this possibly be true? How could any notion of dignity be outside and separate from human diversity? Another implication from Waldron's conception of dignity is the impression that Buddhism, Jainism, Hinduism, and many other cultural and epistemological systems from outside the Western/European world have no conception of dignity that could possibly be superior to our own. We are left with this impression because Waldron never acknowledges such a possibility by making any kind of mention of other conceptions of dignity.

In tying dignity with law, Waldron is assuming that human beings are fundamentally social beings. Our social systems construct and maintain our notions of personhood. This is why Waldron comes back again and again to how hate speech damages our environment, and in doing so harms us. But dignity can also begin on the notion that human beings are ecological beings, or relational beings, or communicational beings. All of these perspectives lend for fundamentally different conceptions of dignity, and in ways that want nothing to do with hate speech laws. From an ecological perspective, dignity comes from the fact that every life is valuable for achieving our prosperity, meaning every life can potentially make an important contribution to our prosperity. In short, every life can be a *butterfly effect.* From a relational perspective, dignity comes from the fact that the condition of my humanity is bound up with the condition of your humanity. To care about my life demands that I care about your life. From a communicational perspective, dignity comes from the fact that no human being can survive or remain sane in isolation. Communication humanizes us. We become human by engaging each other. So others matter. But this is merely the beginning of other ways of framing and defining dignity. Human diversity is always boundless.

Waldron is promoting a shallow conception of dignity. According to Waldron, inclusion demands dignity, and dignity demands laws. But why should dignity be hitched to inclusion? Did the exclusion of African Americans for over 350 years deprive them of their dignity, meaning did such exclusion deprive them of their humanity? Did it undermine their resolve to live honorably, democratically, and charitably? Yet what hate speech is even remotely comparable to over 350 years of slavery, Black codes, and Jim Crow practices? In other words, if hate speech causes harm and injures the dignity and humanity of members of minority groups, then what should 350 years of slavery, Black codes, and Jim Crow practices have done to the dignity of African Americans? In fact, what damage should have 2,500 years of slavery, persecution, discrimination, and the Holocaust done to the dignity of Jews? The dignity of Jews and African Americans reveals that dignity must come from inside of us. It must be forged from inside out. African Americans, Jews, Native Americans, and all other peoples who endured all manner of human evils remind us that no set of words can rob us of our dignity, and to suggest otherwise is an affront to the dignity of these peoples' ancestors.

Finally, Waldron is assuming that certain kinds of language, symbols, and monuments are inherently harmful, and thus should be suppressed for the sake of achieving a well-ordered society. In other words, certain kinds of language inherently and supposedly have the power to hurt and harm. So in Waldron's view, hate speech *incites*, hate speech *dehumanizes*, hate speech *devalues*, hate speech *reinforces*, hate speech *marginalizes*, hate speech *injures*. Apparently, human beings have no capacity to interpret words in different ways, and respond to words in different ways. Words supposedly have all the power. Words can bring us to our knees. But if such is the case, how to explain the endless polls and surveys that show members of the same race, the same tribe, the same gender, the same sexual orientation, the same religion, the same nationality, having opposing views on language, symbols, and monuments that are supposedly hateful? Waldron never broaches this kind of diversity. As Stephen Newman (2017) observes, "Reading Waldron's book one gets the impression that the persons targeted by hatemongers by and large lack the capacity to defend their own dignity" (p. 685). Moreover, "Waldron's account of the harm in hate speech presents us with an emotionally charged portrait of traumatized victims deserving of our sympathy and in dire need of the protection of the censor" (pp. 685-686). Also, in regards to determining what language and symbol is hateful and what the appropriate response should be, why should the view of the majority prevail in any group, especially when history makes no case for the majority being a reliable moral guide?

Waldron claims that the fact that suppressing hate speech will do nothing to end the thoughts driving such speech should be of no concern to us. Some thoughts simply deserve no kind of recognition, and "perhaps it is a good thing to drive race hatred underground, depriving it of the oxygen that it needs in order to flourish" (Waldron, 2012a). But how then are we to know what dangerous thoughts are fomenting below the surface and the forces driving and fortifying these thoughts? How can we address a problem without being able to identify it? We would all prefer to live in a world where there is no humiliation, intimidation, and discrimination against any group, but how could such a world be possible if human beings supposedly have no power to even control what words mean? If words have the power to do all kinds of horrible things to us, then Waldron needs to account for the origins of this power, rather than merely assuming such to be case. That Waldron supports the criminalizing of hate speech means that this account is owed to us in terms of justifying to ourselves the real harm that comes with being found guilty of hate speech offenses.

In a paper titled *The Normativity of Using Prison to Control Hate Speech: The Hollowness of Waldron's Harm Theory*, Dennis Baker and Lucy Shao (2013) contend that criminalizing any kind of speech requires demonstrating measurable harm to an identifiable victim. "We have to be able to measure the harm's impact not against the collective, but against the group member who claims to have been criminally harmed. We have to measure how the denigrating expression about people sharing the victim's ascriptive characteristics such as skin color, obesity, sexual orientation, disability, and so on, has harmfully impacted the victim: that is, psychologically diminished her ability to participate fully in society" (p. 651). Of course to admit to this kind of harm is to reveal that a bigoted person—meaning a person who is morally inferior to you—has the power and means—by merely being able to utter certain words and phrases—to control the quality of your life. In this way, such a confession reveals that hateful words are the least of your concerns. You must now account for why you are allowing such a despicable person to have such control over the quality of your life.

In the end, Waldron believes that suppressing hate speech contributes to the making of a better society by saving us from all the hurt and harm that hate speech causes. Yet there is no agreement on what hate speech is. Every country with hate speech laws has a different definition, and every person certainly has a different definition. This diversity reminds us that human beings, rather than words, mean. We shape what words mean, and how we experience different words. The same words that you experience as violating your dignity and undermining your security, I might experience differently. That we have the power to shape what words mean means that we have the power to shape our lives and ultimately our worlds. Yes, nobody wants to live in a world with hate speech, but the presence of hate speech reminds us that there is still much work to be done. We must remain vigilant. If anything, a well-ordered society should be one that values communication above everything else. Such a society recognizes that communication is the foundation of democracy, and through democracy, diversity rises. As such, a well-ordered society should be one that is always encouraging us to engage each other honestly, patiently, and compassionately. Our goal should be to understand rather than condemn, as in understanding why a person is seeking to harm others, or indifferent to doing so. For Waldron, the argument is between free speech and hate speech. But this is false. The argument is about how best is human flourishing achieved, through regulation or communication?

However, Waldron is by no means the only prominent academic that continues to falsely insist that free speech promotes hate speech, and in doing so undermines diversity and inclusion. According to Judith Butler, Professor in the Department of Comparative Literature and the Program of Critical Theory at the University of California, Berkeley, "If free speech does take precedence over every other constitutional principle and every other community principle, then perhaps we should no longer claim to be weighing or balancing competing principles or values. We should perhaps frankly admit that we have agreed in advance to have our community sundered, racial and sexual minorities demeaned, the dignity of trans people denied, that we are, in effect, willing to be wrecked by this principle of free speech" (quoted in Marantz, 2018, p. 42). As with Waldron, Butler is assuming that words have power because meaning resides in words. Thus for Butler, words can demean, words can wreck, words can sunder, words can deny us our dignity. So in order to stop words from doing all of these ugly things, Butler, as like Waldron, believes that suppressing free speech is vital. However, Butler, as like Waldron, never tells us what moral, cultural, ideological, and epistemological perspective should be used to determine what speech should be suppressed and even criminalized. We should simply assume that suppressing free speech is necessary for protecting members of minority groups from harm, which means assuming that members of minority groups have no capacity to act upon the world independently and in bold ways.

According to Mari J. Matsuda, Charles Lawrence III, Richard Delgado, and Kimberle Williams Crenshaw, authors of *Words that Wound: Critical Race Theory, Assaultive Speech, and the First Amendment*, free speech needs to be seen within a political and historical context that unevenly and unfairly privileges certain voices that, in too many cases, aim to degrade and undermine the views, positions, and experiences of peoples who have been historically marginalized. Thus, free speech simply means giving these privileged voices the wherewithal to continue to abuse and victimize minority peoples. As with Waldron's and Butler's position, this position by Matsuda and company assumes that words have the power to hurt, and thus allowing language to be fully unbridled leaves minority peoples vulnerable to all kinds of abuse under the pretext of free speech. Consequently, the only way to end this kind of abuse, according to this view, is to put strict limits on any language that supposedly causes harm to minority peoples. However, the problem with this argument by Matsuda and company is that no context is ever even and fair to all groups. No doubt, much abuse happens in the name of free speech. But certain perspectives and experiences will always be privileged and encouraged. Moreover, limiting the public expression of certain kinds of speech does nothing to end the motives and reasons that are giving rise to speech that is being judged as "hateful" and "offensive." Also, as with Waldron and Butler, Matsuda and company never tell us who gets to decide what speech should be legally suppressed, and who has the authority to speak on behalf of different minority peoples? In other words, how does any democratic and pluralistic society evenly and fairly decide and adjudicate what speech should be legally suppressed? As David Cole observes in an essay titled *Why We Must Still Defend Free Speech*, "It is easy to recognize inequality; it is virtually impossible to articulate a standard for suppression of speech that would not afford government officials dangerously broad discretion and invite discrimination against particular views." Also, why should minority groups "trust representatives of the majority to decide what speech should be censored?" After all, in most cases, which history evidences, the interests of minority groups have always been in conflict with those of the majority. In fact, hate speech codes were originally used to suppress the speech of minority peoples on college campuses under the claim by White students that

Black students were engaging in racist speech and inviting speakers on campuses who were supposedly guilty of fomenting riots. In the end, Jill Lepore, Professor of History at Harvard University, makes an important point, "All speech is not equal. Some things are true; some things are not." However, "Figuring out how to tell the difference is the work of the university, which rests on a commitment to freedom of inquiry, an unflinching search for truth, and the fearless unmasking of error. . . . Free speech . . . is a long and strenuous argument, as maddening as the past and as painful as the truth."

Free speech poses no harm to members of minority groups. If anything, free speech reminds us that ignorance exists. It saves us from a false civility. It reminds us to be vigilant. On the other hand, free speech also means the protection of speech that threatens the status quo, such as speech that reflects a different rationality, a different sensibility, a different spirituality, a different modality, that in turn reflects different experiences, different struggles, different privileges, different resources, different heritages, and so forth. Free speech means the inability of any group to invoke any kind of pretext to suppress any kind of speech its finds offensive and threatening. In this way, diversity needs free speech in order to flourish. The case that Butler makes for the suppression of free speech is no different to that made by religious regimes to suppress speech. As with Waldron, Butler is merely using diversity and inclusion as a pretext to promote tyranny—one group using arbitrary rationales to justify coercively and hierarchically suppressing different modes of being.

Civility as Inclusion
Inclusion demands the taming, neutralizing, and sterilizing of human diversity. We call this process "civility." We must agree to be

civil to each other, regardless of our differences. We must "agree to disagree without being disagreeable." We must agree to lessen the intensity and ferocity of our differences. We must agree to believe that without taming, neutralizing, and sterilizing our differences, nothing good will become possible. We must therefore agree to believe that in order for diversity to be possible, homogeneity must rule. Diversity must be bound by homogeneity. We must agree to be civil before anything else.

There is no agreement on what "civility" means (Bejan, 2017). However, all that really matters is what civility represents—us believing that without taming, neutralizing, and sanitizing diversity, chaos will supposedly ensue. So in order to achieve any kind of prosperity, human diversity must supposedly be controlled. In this way, civility is about us believing that prosperity demands the submission of human diversity. It represents the necessity of conformity. Being civil means acting like the rest of us, abiding by the same rules, the same norms. Inclusion demands civility. Civility is us agreeing to share the same fears, the same beliefs, the same values. In a word, the same worldview. However, through civility, inclusion undermines human diversity. This is the insidious side of hate speech laws.

We are to assume that hate speech laws represent civility. Civil peoples will supposedly never engage in hate speech, and hate speech laws will supposedly create civility. Thus, the responsibility is on civil peoples to enact laws, such as hate speech laws, that will promote civility. Waldron is consistently making this appeal to us. So again, in order to have inclusion, civility is supposedly necessary, and civility means hate speech laws. This is how Waldron gets to hate speech laws being integral to a well-ordered society. Such a society values civility because such a society values law and order. In fact, civility comes before everything else. Civility dictates what becomes of diversity, in terms of how much diversity and what kinds of diversity. For Waldron, the harm that hate speech causes is to our civility. Hate speech makes us less civil. It threatens and diminishes civility. In other words, hate speech threatens the bonds of homogeneity that are supposedly vital for our prosperity. In reality, Waldron is merely using diversity to make yet another case for civility.

Diversity is the antithesis of civility. Diversity succeeds by harnessing rather than suppressing its intensity and ferocity. That is, diversity succeeds by causing trouble, by disrupting everything, by pushing us to look anew at everything. This is how diversity functions as a life catalyst. It succeeds by promoting possibility, which it does by undermining dominant moral, ideological, and epistemological systems. Any taming of diversity diminishes its ability to do this important life renewing work. Such is the threat that civility poses to diversity. The reality is that hate speech laws have nothing to do with diversity. In fact, hate speech poses no threat to diversity. Diversity will always encounter hate speech. However, hate speech never made for over 350 years of slavery, Black codes, and Jim Crow practices. Neither is hate speech responsible for the mass incarceration of African Americans for nonviolent offenses. Neither is hate speech responsible for the growing gap between rich and poor, the proliferation of weapons of mass destruction, and the ecological peril that is now upon us. In fact, all of these conditions and situations are creatures of systems, structures, and institutions that value civility. Hate speech is merely speech that reveals the ignorance of the person uttering such speech. A world without hate speech is one that is devoid of systems, structures, and institutions that block diversity in the name of civility.

For Teresa Bejan (2017), author of *Mere Civility: Disagreement and the Limits of Toleration,* civility is "the minimum standard of behavior needed to keep a disagreement going" (p. 152). Determining what is this minimum involves answering the following questions: "(1) how much difference can we bear, (2) how much must we share in order to make that difference bearable, and (3) where should we draw the line?" (p. 152). A call for civility "is thus a call for restraint on the basis of something shared, a common ground or a conversational standard the speaker believes to be binding on all parties despite their differences" (p. 152). Like Waldron, Bejan is assuming that one person's humanity is outside and separate from another person's humanity. So in order for us to get along, we supposedly need to agree on a set of minimum rules. For Bejan, "The importance of having a shared way of doing things—as a precondition of predictability, mutual expectation, and trust—is obvious. Without it social life in tolerant societies, especially, would be impossible" (p. 152).

The challenge for civility is determining and agreeing on what needs to be shared. However, from an ecological perspective, or a relational perspective, or a communicational perspective, what is shared *is* already shared as there is no separation between human being. The challenge for diversity is getting us to recognize this fact, and thus appreciating how the condition of my humanity is bound up with the condition of your humanity. To impede my flourishing is to impede yours. In short, civility and diversity are of different views of the human experience. If my humanity is outside and separate from your humanity, or I am perceiving such to be the case, then you become much more of a stranger to me. I am more inclined to be suspicious of you, even to be afraid of you. Civility becomes détente. It contains our suspicions of each other's differences. So rather than inclusion, Bejan believes that the goal of civility is toleration. It is about determining the minimum amount of difference we can tolerate.

However, when I assume no separation between us, I am less inclined to be afraid of you and your differences. I am therefore more inclined to engage you and even be vulnerable to you. This, in fact, is where diversity begins. It begins where communication begins, in our being vulnerable to each other. In being vulnerable to each other we recognize ourselves in each other. In other words, rather than sowing division and separation, diversity promotes union and communion. As we recognize more and more of our-selves in each other as we become more and more vulnerable to each other, we also recognize how different we are as a result of our different experiences, different heritages, different resources, dif-ferent influences, different environments, and different struggles. Vulnerability highlights our diversity. How much diversity we are capable of creating and generating will therefore depend on how vulnerable we are capable of becoming. That diversity is bound up with communication reminds us that diversity is never one thing. Instead, through communication diversity is always changing and evolving, always becoming different.

Conclusion

In a statement to the *Washington Post* after the students were found guilty and suspended, Syracuse University said that The Theta Tau videos "had a significant impact on the well-being of students, fac-ulty and staff on this campus and in the greater university commu-nity. The videos contain language, even if offered under the guise of satire, that is sexist, racist, ableist, anti-Semitic and demeaning to the LGTBQ community. . . . Moreover, speech or conduct can be harassing in nature based on its effect on others, even if it was not the underlying purpose or intent." But Syracuse University is yet to reveal how this "significant impact" was measured or deter-mined, including what science or scholarly method the university used to do so. It also continues to insist that meaning is found in words and that intent has no place in communication, even when these false assumptions make a mockery of foundational tenets in communication theory, and nearly everything found in introductory communication courses, including those offered at Syracuse University. As Lyell Asher (2018), a professor of English at Lewis & Clark College, reminds us, "Satire, irony, parody — these are things we teach. [And] none exists without respect for intention."

As for words causing harm, Scott O. Lillienfeld, a Professor of Psychology at Emory University, found negligible support in a comprehensive study of different scholarly literatures in psychology for any of the core assumptions that made for the rise of microaggressions. Consequently, Lillienfeld calls for an abandoning of the label "microaggression" and a moratorium on microaggression training on college campuses until scholarship emerges that supports the notion. For Lillienfeld, the methodological problem deals with intention, interpretation, and reaction as what constitutes a microaggression is in the eye of the beholder. Human diversity means that all human beings interpret things differently. What one person may view as a microaggression (e.g., "You speak so eloquently.") another may view as a compliment. Indeed, the notion that "Some kinds of free speech really can be harmful" has no basis in science or history. No proponent of "hate speech" proscriptions is yet to give any kind of account of how "hate speech" *actually* causes harm. We are merely to assume that because language has power, hateful language has the power to do hateful things.

However, any power that language has comes from us. We decide and determine what words mean and how words impact us. Words have power *only* when we choose to give words power. As such, no word is inherently offensive. Human beings use words to hurt people. If there is ever going to be a world without hate, this will only be possible by stopping people from becoming hateful rather than criminalizing hate speech. Only when people are no longer hateful will hate speech end. What language politics is really about is taming our differences for the sake of achieving uniformity and conformity. It has nothing to do with diversity. Diversity is merely a pretext for conformity. Language politics is all about preserving the status quo, as in reinforcing the belief that without the imposition of order and hierarchy (e.g., hate speech rules, speech codes, language covenants), our society will descend into chaos and anarchy and minority peoples will be traumatized and excluded. So for the sake of preserving order and diversity, rules and laws are necessary, which also means that institutional apparatuses like a Chief Diversity Officer, Department of Multiculturalism, Department of Public Safety, Office of Equal Opportunity, Inclusion, and Resolution Services, being necessary to impose these rules and laws.

Once again inclusion succeeds by peddling an illusion. In this case, that meaning resides in words. In promoting and reinforcing this illusion, we convince ourselves that *not* only language must be controlled, but ultimately we must be controlled. Diversity, again, is merely the pretext for control. But control is supposedly necessary for us to refrain from hurting others with our words. So when any deviancy occurs, our rules and regulations must be vigorously enforced. That language supposedly contains meaning means our locus of control is outside of us. We are controlled by outside forces. We can supposedly do nothing about the fact that language can harm us. Language has power. We supposedly have nothing.

That certain language can supposedly harm us means that institutions are necessary to save us from such harm, and successfully do so by imposing rules and regulations on us. In this way, inclusion succeeds by convincing us that we have no capacity to control ourselves and achieve harmony with each other without a vast system of rules and regulations. We must be controlled from the outside to achieve a harmony that assumes as such. As long as we accept this premise, or this view of the human experience, then what kind of rules, what kind of regulations, and what kind of sentences an institution imposes on us become secondary.

Finally, for all the commotion about what language should be suppressed and banned for the supposed sake of promoting diversity and inclusion, let us note that there is no moment in history that shows language politics being responsible for changing the course of history. The end of slavery, Jim Crow practices, apartheid in South Africa, the Holocaust, had nothing to do with language politics. Instead, these horrors came to an end through struggle and sacrifice. Further, there is no evidence that language politics is bringing about social and political change. Instead, the threat of sanction, humiliation, and retribution for using "offensive" language only seems to be making for a false civility and collegiality. That a person is now disallowed from publicly saying certain things does nothing to change what the person honestly feels and still says behind closed doors. If anything, language politics seems to be only succeeding in suppressing the kind of honest and difficult communication that comes with dealing with and getting past many wrenching social, racial, and political issues.

CHAPTER 4
DIVERSITY, INCLUSION & HARM

The judicial board adjudicating the hearing at Syracuse University said the satirical skits threatened the mental health, physical health, and safety of people who sought out and viewed the videos of the event. However, the board provided no science to support this extraordinary claim that no doubt played an important role in its deliberations and final ruling. How was the board able to get away with making this assumption in an institution of higher learning, especially when the consequences would be very real for the accused students? Yet colleges and universities are by no means the only place that believes that certain words can cause harm.

Recently, Google fired James Damore, a software engineer, for using language that it judged to be inherently offensive. Google issued a statement to employees that identically resembled those issued by Syracuse University. Titled "Our Words Matter," Google said that Damore's words had violated the company's code of conduct "by advancing harmful gender stereotypes in our workplace." It also said that Damore' words had "clearly impacted our co-workers," some of whom were hurt and felt "judged based on their gender."

Damore's words were judged to be "offensive" and "contrary to our basic values." Also, like Syracuse University, Google framed the controversy as that between provocative speech and offensive speech. On one hand, Google wants "Googlers" to "feel free to express dissent" and raise "important topics." However, Googlers must do so in ways that conform to "our Code of Conduct." For Google, the challenge is finding "a way to debate issues on which we might disagree—while doing so in line with our Code of Conduct." This is supposedly necessary for creating "a more inclusive environment for all." In another statement to employees, Google said that "part of building an open, inclusive environment means fostering a culture in which those with alternative views, including different political views, feel safe sharing their opinions. But that discourse needs to work alongside the principles of equal employment found in our Code of Conduct, policies, and anti-discrimination laws."

But how does immediately terminating people who are merely perceived to be offensive help Google promote robust debate, especially when Google is the final decider of when provocative speech becomes offensive speech? Why also is Google assuming that punitive action is necessary for achieving diversity and inclusion? How does the threat of termination promote communication, and what comfort can Googlers take in Google's promise to take no "action against anyone for promoting" discussions that reflect a minority viewpoint? No doubt, Google is assuming that meaning resides in words, as in casually claiming that Damore's words were "advancing harmful stereotypes" and "clearly impacted our co-workers." In uttering words that Google judged to be inherently offensive, Damore was judged to be offensive, and thus had to be fired. Google's point in immediately firing Damore is that persons who supposedly use offensive language have no place at Google. However, like Syracuse University, Google offers no science to explain the nature of offensive speech. We are merely to assume that there is such a thing, and it is obvious to all.

But what exactly was James Damore's intent, a notion, again, that is foundational in communication theory? Was Damore intentionally seeking to be offensive and cause harm? In other words, why did Google have no interest in knowing Damore's intent? In the end, Google is contending that intent has no significant place in communication. But again, from the standpoint of communication theory, this is folly. Gerald Miller and Mark Steinberg, authors of *Between People: A New Analysis Of Interpersonal Communication*, define communication as "an intentional, transactional, symbolic process." The reason being, claim Miller and Steinberg, is that "intent to communicate and intent to influence are synonymous. If there is no intent, there is no message." For Richard West and Lynn Turner, authors of *Introducing Communication Theory: Analysis and Application*, without intent, the study of communication becomes impossible. "If everything can be thought of as communication—our verbal and nonverbal unintended expressions—then studying communication in a systematic manner is not only challenging but nearly impossible. . . . By defining everything as communication, we inevitably undermine the field we wish to study." Intent means that our communication should be measured solely by our intention. It also means that people have the ability to act deliberately. So whereas to view communication in terms of language and symbols is to assume that the *impact* of our communication is what is important, to define communication in terms of meaning ("Yes, I know what you said, but what exactly did you mean?") is to assume that the *intent* of our communication is important.

Also, why did Google assume that Damore was devoid of empathy and compassion in terms of choosing what words to utter? In other words, where was the element of grace in Google's handling of this matter? Grace is another important notion in communication theory because there is simply no reliable way for us to know exactly what another person means. Also, what of the many women who stridently disagreed with Google's handling of this matter, such as the woman who said in a *New York Times post*, "I am a woman. I am offended by the Google CEO's decision that women can't cope with offensive stereotypes put forth by a fellow employee, as demonstrated by its dismissal of Mr. Damore. I've been doing it all my life (72 years) and have been made stronger by the challenge of dealing with misogyny. Firing a person because you don't like what he says dampens creativity and the free flow of ideas. [Google] made a bad decision." Or another woman who said in another *New York Times* post, "This firing makes me squirm. . . . I am a female scientist and have experienced first-hand discrimination because of my gender. . . . I think sitting [Damore] down with female engineers who could tell him their personal journeys would be a better approach. Provide him with a male mentor who understands that women do experience roadblocks just because of their sex. Educate him on what it would be like if he were female. It's possible that he would maintain his beliefs. However, with his firing this opportunity to open his eyes is lost." Or Jodie Ginsberg, of the Index on Censorship, who said, "I think it's wrong for a company to fire someone for simply expressing their opinion. . . . [The] message [Google] is sending is that people are not free to express their beliefs and opinions. . . . A much better way is to discuss those opinions openly."

What does such diversity of perspectives among women reveal about Google's supposed commitment to diversity and inclusion? In fact, what does such diversity reveal about the purchase of Google's definition of diversity? In the end, Google is reinforcing a shallow definition of diversity. We being of different races, genders, and sexual orientations only represent the beginning of human diversity. There is also diversity in our different sensibilities, our different rationalities, our different modalities, our different spiritualities, our different ideologies, our different cosmologies, our different epistemologies, which in turn reflect our different backgrounds, our different experiences, our different circumstances, our different struggles, our different opportunities, our different resources, and our different privileges.

Human diversity is really about human complexity. No group—regardless of how stable we assume and desire it to be—will ever be of one truth, one perspective, one reality, one morality, one meaning, one politics, or one anything. Yet this axiom is what brings the study of communication into focus. Assuming undermines communicating. Google had no business assuming that *all* women were of one reality, one truth, one perspective. For the sake of diversity, Google would have been better off doing much more communicating, which would have involved Google doing much less judging, shaming, and condemning before assuming to know James Damore's intent and meaning.

Problems with a Discipline

The notion that certain words have the power to hurt and harm reflects a limited view of the human experience. It reflects a view that assumes that causation is fundamentally about forces acting upon matter. We supposedly have no agency, no capacity to shape our lives by our own choices. In this backward view of the human experience, drugs cause addiction, pornography causes deviancy, poverty causes criminality, and so forth. However, this kind of assessment of causation has no basis in modern science. Yet this limited view of the human experience still pervades communication studies. The focus is still essentially on learning to speak persuasively rather than to listen compassionately. Indeed, I am yet to find a communication curriculum that has a public listening course, and a foundational communication textbook that focuses evenly on speaking and listening. Instead, the focus remains on using language persuasively and effectively so as to achieve desired goals and outcomes.

We still assume in communication studies that communication is fundamentally a linguistic and symbolic phenomenon. Human beings, claims Kenneth Burke, are a "symbol-using, symbol-making, and symbol-misusing animal." We create symbols to name things and situations, to relate to other human beings and things, and to manipulate and take advantage of others. For Mark V. Redmond, "Symbols are probably the single most important quality that gives us our humanness, separating us from all other animals. Without symbols no other human creation is possible. Symbols allow us to remember and reminisce, to evaluate and plan, to coordinate, to communicate abstract thoughts, to think about the future, and to consider alternatives and outcomes." James W. Neuliep (2015), author of *Intercultural Communication: A Contextual Approach*, writes, "Human communication—that is, the ability to symbolize and use language—separates humans from animals. Communication with others is the essence of what it means to be human" (p. 10). For Joel Charon, "It is the symbol that translates the world from the physical sensed reality to a reality that can be understood, dissected, integrated, and tested. Between reality and what we see and do stands the symbol. Once we learn symbols we are in a position of understanding our environment rather than simply responding to it, and once that happens what we come to see and act on is colored by our symbols." For J. W. Carey, "Communication is a symbolic process whereby reality is produced, maintained, repaired, and transformed." Moreover, through language and other symbolic forms, communication "comprises the ambience of human existence." For C. David Mortensen, "language, conflict, and communication initially arose from pressures built in to the critical life-or-death situations our ancestors were compelled to share with one another. From such a perspective, communication is viewed as a world-analyzing, reality-testing, survival-oriented mechanism. Complex language enables humans to transform the cultural inheritance and fulfill basic ecological tasks associated with individual security and collective well-being." According to Daniel C. Dennett (1994), Director for the Center of Cognitive Studies at Tufts University, "We human beings may not be the most admirable species on the planet, or the most likely to survive another millennium, but we are without any doubt at all the most intelligent. We are also the only species with language" (p. 161). In *Descent of Man*, Charles Darwin said that "articulate language was peculiar to man" and also a reliable measure of distinguishing "civilized races" from "savage races."

To assume that communication is fundamentally a linguistic and symbolic process is to also assume that communication emerges when both encoder (sender) and decoder (receiver) share a common linguistic and symbolic system. Communication supposedly demands inclusion. We supposedly have to put aside our differences for the sake of communication. In order for communication to rise, inclusion must rule. Moreover, because communication supposedly gives us order, agreement, and unity, inclusion becomes integral to human flourishing. It supposedly saves us from the ravages of chaos, disagreement, and disunity. If communication makes everything good, inclusion supposedly makes everything better.

According to the National Communication Association, which "advances Communication as the discipline that studies all forms, modes, media, and consequences of communication through humanistic, social scientific, and aesthetic inquiry," communication is a *transactional process* that is inherently symbolic in nature. "A communicator encodes (for example, puts thoughts into words and gestures), then transmits the message via a channel (for example, speaking, email, text message) to the other communicator(s) who then decode the message (for example, take the words and apply meaning to them). The message may encounter noise, which could prevent the message from being received or fully understood as the sender intended." In communication studies, noise refers to anything that interferes in the accuracy of shared meaning. According to Joseph DeVito, author of the book *Messages: Building Interpersonal Communication Skills*, "Noise enters all communication systems, no matter how well designed. Noise is anything that distorts or interferes with the reception of messages. It is present in a communication system to the extent that the message received differs from the message sent." Noise supposedly promotes confusion. We supposedly achieve communication by removing confusion. In *Intercultural Communication: A Reader*, Edwin R. McDaniel refers to language diversity as a "distraction." According to McDaniel, "For effective communication in an intercultural interaction, participants must rely on a common language." One person using a different language "can adversely affect the receiver's understanding of the message." Simply put, in order for communication to be possible, homogeneity rather than diversity must rule. Both persons sharing the same language supposedly facilitates feedback, which is supposedly the most integral component in any communication system. It is "the information sent to an entity (an individual or a group) about its prior behavior so that the entity may adjust its current and future behavior to achieve the desired result."

Feedback supposedly allows us to correct and control our messages. It makes convergence possible, thereby supposedly making communication possible. Feedback supposedly allows us to move from divergence to convergence. Presumably, communication is about achieving convergence, as in moving from chaos to order. For Edward Brewer and Jim Westerman, "Communication is . . . simply necessary for creating order out of chaos" (p. 3). Stephen W. Littlejohn claims that *convergence theory* and *information theory* help explain why there is similarity within groups and differences between them, or why groups that share more achieve more convergence, and those that share less achieve less divergence. Littlejohn explains, "As communication decreases, the amount of variation within a group increases, the structure of the system comes apart, and entropy prevails. As communication increases within a group, more and more is shared, structure develops, and convergence results. Generally speaking then, the more communication, the greater the convergence, and the less the communication, the greater the divergence. People within a group come to share common ideas as they communicate with greater frequency, and they come to lose common ground when they communicate less frequently." In this way, communication from the perspective of the National Communication Association cultivates a valuing of conformity and homogeneity by promoting the notion that communication needs commonality (such as sharing common experiences, common backgrounds, common ambitions, common struggles, common training) in order to succeed. Indeed, viewing communication from the perspective of language and symbols assumes that divergence (noise and difference) threatens communication and all that communication supposedly makes possible, such as unity, prosperity, and progress. We supposedly achieve communication by removing divergence (noise and difference), and in achieving communication "common ground" occurs. Thus to view communication from the perspective of language and symbols is to be about developing theories, strategies, and technologies that will allow us to either limit or avoid divergence (noise and difference). Ultimately, the notion of communication as fundamentally linguistic and symbolic process reflects a racial, ideological, political, cultural, and epistemological hegemon that views divergence (difference) as a threat to all that is presumably good, such as, to use Littlejohn's words, "common ground."

However, no great civilization has ever been linguistically, or even racially, religiously, politically, ideologically homogenous.

Every great civilization is a creature of both convergence (order and assimilation) and divergence (chaos and immigration). Just as well, communication needs both convergence and divergence. Divergence challenges us to look at things anew. It makes change possible by disrupting the order of things. We now refer to this process of disrupting the order of things as *divergent thinking*— thinking about things in ways that disrupt the order of things and makes new things possible. Albert Einstein was divergent. Louise Michel was divergent. Martin Luther King, Jr., was divergent. Duke Ellington was divergent. Nikola Tesla was divergent. John Lennon was divergent. Mark Twain was divergent. Harriett Tubman was divergent. Janis Joplin was divergent.

From Language to Meaning

Rather than viewing communication in terms of language and symbols, a much more heuristic and constructive way of viewing communication is in terms of meaning. To view communication from the perspective of meaning is to assume that human beings are foremost meaning-making beings rather than symbol-making, symbol-using beings. We strive to make sense of things, to give meaning to things. Creating, sharing, and contesting meaning is what human beings do. Life unfolds through meaning, and through meaning life becomes different things to different peoples. In *Man's Search For Meaning*, Viktor Frankl claims that "Man's search for meaning is the primary motivation in his life." We find meaning, or at least any that can sustain us, by turning outward, by engaging the world and each other honestly and transparently. According to Frankl, human beings find meaning in three different ways: "(1) by creating a work or doing a deed; (2) by experiencing something or encountering someone; and (3) by the attitude we take toward unavoidable suffering." The quality of our meaning will depend on how much we are capable of turning outward, thereby becoming completely open to the world and each other. Examples of this outward turning would be honesty and transparency. Both of these things heighten life's intensity and richness by pushing us to deal with the world on its own terms and conditions. Frankl contends that through the pursuit of meaning human beings achieve the means to transform our worlds and our lives. According to Frankl, "man . . . determines himself whether he gives in to conditions or stands up to them. In other words, man is ultimately self-determining. Man does not simply exist but always decides what his existence will be, what he will become in the next moment. . . . Man is capable of changing the world for the better if possible, and of changing himself for the better if necessary." We decide and determine what will become of us by the meaning we create of things. Moreover, because all human beings have different experiences and must deal with different challenges with different resources, what one thing means to one person can be fundamentally different to what it means to another. On the other hand, there is nothing that limits what anything can mean to any person, which is to say that such limits are purely of our own making. "The important point to remember," writes Lee Thayer (2011) in *Explaining Things: Inventing Ourselves and Our Worlds*, "is that *nothing* we encounter in the world—including words and images—contains or conveys meaning. It is we humans who provide that in every instance. What something means is not what that something means, but what it means to the person making the interpretation of some aspect of the world" (p. 104). Thus for Thayer, "Communication is first of all about interpretations. Nothing comes to us with its meaning inscribed on its back. What something means to you or to me is found in interpretation." However, because all human beings are of different experiences, different backgrounds, different resources, different tribulations, different perspectives, and different circumstances, our interpretations tend to be consistently different. Communication is about sharing, navigating, and challenging our different interpretations of different things. For Deanna L. Fassett, John T. Warren, and Keith Nainby (2018), authors of *Communication: A Critical/Cultural Introduction*, "communication is the collaborative construction and negotiation of meaning between self and others as it occurs within cultural contexts" (p. 11).

To view communication from the perspective of meaning is to believe that meaning is what *really* matters in communication. In other words, communication is about determining what meanings are emerging. "Yes, I know what you said, but what exactly do you mean?" Alternatively, "Yes, I know what I said, but that is not what I meant." Many different things shape and influence what things mean to different people. In order to understand what I mean, you have to pay attention to many different things. In fact, determining what any person means is difficult and complex as our experiences and worldviews can be fundamentally different. There is simply no way to know precisely what a person means. Consequently, communication requires restraint, generosity, and grace. We should give others the benefit of the doubt and be generous in our interpretations of things. We should even be ready to be wrong. From the perspective of meaning, communication is "the process by which people interactively create, sustain, and manage meaning." Or, "communication is a process of creating a meaning between two or more people." For W. Barnett Pearce, communication arises from our coordinating and managing our meaning. "Communication is about meaning . . . but not just in a passive sense of perceiving messages. Rather, we live in lives filled with meaning and one of our life challenges is to manage those meaning so that we can make our social worlds coherent and live within them with honor and respect. But this process of managing our meaning is never done in isolation. We are always and necessarily coordinating the way we manage our meaning with other people."

To view communication from the perspective of meaning is to assume that meaning resides within human beings rather than in language and symbols. The study of communication is *really* the study of human beings and the relationships between human beings that make different kinds of meaning possible. What forces, experiences, and relationships shape our meaning of things? Why do certain things (like the Second Amendment to the US Constitution—"A well regulated Militia, being necessary to the security of a free State, the right of the people to keep and bear Arms, shall not be infringed") mean different things to different people? What social and political consequences come from different meaning and the relationships that make for different meaning? As Mikhail Bakhtin notes, "there is no reason for saying that meaning belongs to a word as such. In essence, meaning belongs to a word in its position between speakers; that is, meaning is realized only in the process of active, responsive understanding. Meaning does not reside in the word or in the soul of the speaker or in the soul of the listener. Meaning is the *effect of interaction between speaker and listener produced via the material of a particular sound complex*" (p. 35). On the other hand, to claim that human beings impose meaning on things is by no mean to deny that human beings use things to preserve meaning. As Mark Johnson (2007) explains,

> Meaning requires a functioning brain, in a living body that engages its environments—environments that are social and cultural, as well as physical and biological. Cultural artifacts and practices—for example, language, architecture, music, art, ritual acts, and public institutions—preserve aspects of meaning as objective features of this world. Without these cultural artifacts, our accumulated meaning, understanding, and knowledge would not be preserved over time, and each new generation would have to literally start over from scratch. . . . However, we must keep in mind

that those sociocultural objects, practices, and events are not meaningful in themselves. Rather they become meaningful only insofar as they are enacted in the lives of human beings who *use* the language, *live* by the symbols, *sing* and *appreciate* the music, *participate* in the rituals, and *reenact* the practices and values of institutions. (p. 152)

To view communication from the perspective of meaning is to assume that our meanings are always different because our origins, experiences, resources, and circumstances are always different. Thus, what one thing means to one person can be fundamentally different to what it means to another. For example, what being a Muslim means to one person can be completely different to what it means to another person. As Abdolkarim Soroush, a prominent scholar of Islam, acknowledges, "The essence of religion will always be sacred, but its interpretation by fallible human beings is not sacred—and therefore can be criticized, modified, refined, and redefined. What single person can say what God meant? Any fixed version would effectively smother religion. It would block the rich exploration of the sacred texts. Interpretations are also influenced by the age you live in, by the conditions and mores of the era, and by other branches of that knowledge. So there's no single, inflexible, or absolute interpretation of Islam for all time." Indeed, nothing, even religious scriptures, lends for only one meaning. Yet this in no way means that all interpretations are equally valid. It merely means that there is always the possibility of a different meaning.

To view communication from the perspective of meaning is to switch the focus of communication away from the sender to the receiver. In popular understandings of communication, the focus is on the sender (or the encoder). This is plainly seen in Public Speaking (rather than Public Listening) courses being mandatory in communication programs and departments. The focus is on being fluent and eloquent, making rigorous and compelling arguments, and presenting information that seduces and appeals to different audiences. We assume that the sender plays the primary role in any communication situation. It is the sender who supposedly has the ability and the means to make various things possible. Using language and symbols, the sender conveys, the sender persuades, the sender propagates, the sender shapes, the sender calibrates, the sender imposes, and the sender manipulates. Consequently, language politics is all about blaming and accusing the sender of being offensive. The problem is always with the sender. It is always the sender's fault. However, from the perspective of meaning, the receiver is who is really important. It is the receiver who will ultimately decide what things mean. As Lee Thayer explains, "A person may be listening to you. But what that person is hearing is not what you said, but her own interpretation of what you may (or may not) have said. All the actual consequences of any communication encounter flow from the interpretations that people make of things. That may or may not be what you intended. But the power player in any communication situation is the *receiver*, not the *sender*." As such, "All consequences flow from how the receiver interprets things." To view communication from the perspective of meaning is to view power as residing within the realm of interpretation rather than the realm of transmission or persuasion. That I have the ability to shape what things mean means that I have the ability to control how I respond to things and persons, and how I allow either to impact me. It also means that I am responsible for how I choose to respond to things as all interpretations have implications and consequences. So regardless of what the sender intends, what the receiver interprets matters.

To view communication from the perspective of meaning is to value the tension between intention and interpretation. Our words, actions, and decisions will always be open to different interpretations. We will never be able to completely or perfectly control how others choose to interpret our words, actions, and decisions. On the other hand, others will never be capable of reliably knowing our intentions and motivations, or the reasons behind our words, actions, and decisions. Consequently, both sides (the side of interpretation, and the side of intention) will always make mistakes and misjudgments. Yet these mistakes and misjudgments form the natural rhythm of communication, just as how waves form the natural rhythm of oceans. Communication will never be perfect, never be correct. We will always be making mistakes and misjudgments. In this way, the flourishing of communication demands grace, patience, and forbearance. We will never be able to perfectly control the realm of interpretation, nor the realm of intention. Yet embracing these limitations enriches communication by pushing us to recognize that our words, actions, and decisions, regardless of our most strenuous efforts, will always be susceptible to all manner of interpretations. Consequently, caution is necessary. We must always be sensitive to the possibility of an interpretation that is beyond our imagination, which again reminds us of why grace, patience, and forbearance are necessary for the flourishing of communication. On the other hand, the best that any person could offer of our words, actions, and decisions are interpretations. Our interpretations are nothing but our own creations, reflecting our biases, beliefs, values, fears, and suspicions. Simply put, interpretations are human things. We promote and vitalize communication by recognizing the limits of our interpretations and always examining the forces and experiences that are shaping and influencing our own meaning of things.

To view communication from the perspective of meaning is to define the study of communication as how human beings create, navigate, coordinate, manage, and challenge meaning. This is supposedly the hallmark of the human experience: us creating, navigating, and challenging meaning. To view the study of communication from the perspective of meaning is to believe that the study of communication should focus on how social and institutional forces impact the creation and propagation of different meanings. In other words, to view communication in terms of meaning is to believe that the study of communication should focus on all the forces, structures, and institutions that affect how human beings make, share, and propagate meaning. How exactly do we arrive at our meaning of things and persons, and what forces encourage or discourage the rise of various meanings?

To view communication from the perspective of meaning is to believe that meaning is always in flux, always moving, shifting, and changing. What I mean this morning can be different from what I mean this evening. Indeed, our meanings are always shifting and changing because of all kinds of forces. When our experiences change, our meanings tend to change. When our contexts change, our meanings tend to change. When our resources change, our meanings tend to change. When our circumstances change, our meanings tend to change. When our environments change, our meanings tend to change. As David Bohm explains in *Unfolding Meaning*, "There is an inherent ambiguity in any concrete meaning. That is to say, how meanings arise and what they signify depends to a large extent on what a given situation means to us, and this may vary according to our interests and motivations, our backgrounds of knowledge, and so on." Simply put, as we change, our meanings change. That meaning is always in flux means that assumptions are a problem in communication. From the perspective of meaning, communication involves cultivating a mind that is vigilant about our assumptions so that communication is never compromised by assumptions. Such a mind is always probing, contesting, and challenging the assumptions that others and ourselves make. Indeed, failing to notice our assumptions makes us intellectually and emotionally lazy, undermining our ability to be open to new meaning of things and persons.

To view communication from the perspective of meaning is about approximation. Even though I will never know for certain what you mean, and you will never know for certain what I mean, all that matters is that we have a good sense of what each other means. That communication is about approximation means that communication will never be complete and absolute. We will always be guessing, triangulating, and approximating. This again is why being generous in our descriptions and interpretations of things and persons is important to achieving communication. In most cases, communication problems arise from a lack of generosity rather than from our failure to correctly guess each other's meaning. On the other hand, to view communication from the perspective of meaning is to believe that our communication problems arise from our failure to create a shared meaning. This can supposedly happen because our perspectives are different, our experiences are different, our assumptions are different, our expectations are different, or our intentions are different. In other words, from the perspective of communication as meaning, our communication problems have nothing much to do with language and symbols. Many factors can obstruct our coming to a shared meaning, such as our unwillingness to listen—truly listen—to things that are difficult and probably unfair. As Alphonso Lingis (1994) notes, "To enter into conversation with another is to lay down one's arms and one'defenses; to throw open the gates of one's own positions; to expose oneself to the other, the outsider; and to lay oneself open to surprises, contestation, and inculpation." To view communication from the perspective of meaning is to recognize that communication is often difficult and demanding. It involves an enormous amount of work and effort as achieving a shared meaning can be difficult.

To view communication from the perspective of meaning is to believe that meaning and context are bound up with each other. Meaning shape contexts, and contexts shape meaning. To know our meaning of things involves knowing the context that is situating and locating our meaning. Communication problems supposedly arise from our failure to properly understand the context that is locating our meaning. But interpreting any context is difficult. To begin with, there are different kinds of contexts. There can be a racial context, a relational context, a cultural context, an historical context, and even a personal context. There is no way to know exactly what context is in play. Also, what I conceive and perceive to be the proper context can be different from what you conceive and perceive to be the proper context. Contexts also mean that what I find to be appropriate can be different from what you find to be appropriate. Finally, contexts are fleeting and always changing. Because contexts are always changing, meanings are always changing. In this regard, context presents many challenges to communication with regards to knowing what a person means. This is why restraint is important in communication. We should emphasize probing and exploring rather than assuming and concluding: "*What exactly did you mean by that?*" Rather than, "*How could you say something so offensive?*" In many ways the problem of communication is the problem of context. We attend to communication by attending to context. Finally, because context shapes meaning, who decides what is the proper or correct context possesses power. That is, power resides with the person who decides what is the right place and time to say certain things. However, such power is always arbitrary as the determination of context is shaped purely by human beings, and has nothing to do with the workings of the natural world. In the end, understanding the nature of context is about recognizing and remembering the following: First, *context is multifaceted*. That is, context has many different dimensions (racial, cultural, political, historical, social, temporal, geographical), which means that any word or symbol, in being bound by context, can always lend for all kinds of different and conflicting meaning. Second, *context is indeterminate*. That is, there is simply no way for different persons to know what context is in play or governing the situation for the other person. What things mean to one person could mean something different to another. Finally, *context is political*. That is, context is always serving an ideological master. Who determines what is the appropriate time and space to say anything has power. Yet upon what legitimate basis is such power achieved?

To view communication from the perspective of meaning is to believe that any meaning-making process is also an identity-making process and a reality-making process. In creating meaning we create ourselves and our social worlds. Consequently, our conceptions and perceptions of ourselves and our worlds are bound up with how we conceive and experience communication. Problems that pertain to our conceptions of ourselves are fundamentally communication problems. Indeed, a popular misconception is that our identity is stable and bound by boxes (*"I am a White, heterosexual, Jewish, woman."*). However, what being White means to one person can be fundamentally different for other persons. Likewise, what being heterosexual means to one person can be fundamentally different for other persons. Likewise, what being Jewish means to one person can be different for other persons. Likewise, what being of a certain gender means to one person can be different for other persons. In short, there is no one definition of any identity marker. Through communication we form our conceptions of ourselves, which is to say that through communication we recognize what things *mean* to us and which people matter to us. This is the stuff of identity, our recognizing the things and people that matter to us. However, as time and space change, these things and people change. So the woman who is a mother today was a daughter many years ago, and the person who is now the

President of an international bank was an environmental activist in school. Times change, people change. Circumstances change, people change. Environments change, people change. So as our lives change because of the changing nature of time and space, how we perceive, describe, and experience ourselves also change. Social problems are also fundamentally communication problems, which means that fixing any social problem involves changing the communication that surrounds that problem. Indeed, no social problem falls from the sky. Certain things must be defined, constituted, and languaged as social problems. There must also be agreement on what constitutes a social problem, and such agreement is achieved through communication. In short, all of these processes happen in communication and belong to a certain kind of communication ecology. No social problem is ever outside or separate from a certain kind of communication ecology. What one society can view as a social problem can *mean* nothing in another society.

To view communication from the perspective of meaning is to recognize that our meanings are always being contested and challenged. There will never be consensus on what things mean as, again, our origins, experiences, and circumstances will always be different. For example, what does being civil mean? What does being offensive mean? What does being a good teacher mean? What does being a good student mean? What does being a feminist mean? What does being a Christian mean? What does being a Muslim mean? What does being an American mean? Instead, what is always at work are attempts and initiatives to create the impression that various things only convey, and can only convey, one meaning. Enter the notion of the *ideograph*. It is tool of ideology, used to sustain and protect the hegemony of a certain kind of ideology. An ideograph is an abstraction, born purely from a system of beliefs, fears, and values that seeks to foster a certain way of viewing and experiencing the world. Ideographs "function as guides, warrants, reasons, or excuses for behavior." The purpose of an ideograph is to have us all share a common set of meanings, and thus a common ideology (a common system of beliefs, values, fears, ambitions, norms) that reinforces a certain hegemony or hegemon. Indeed, ideographs are ideological trojan horses. Inclusion is an ideograph. It is simply and generally assumed to be a good and necessary thing. But where did the notion of inclusion come from? Who gets to decide what inclusion means, and who and what gets to be included? Human diversity is about diversity of experiences, diversity of circumstances, diversity of perspectives, and diversity of meaning. In sum, viewing communication in terms of meaning promotes a pluralistic and democratic sensibility. There is always a recognition and appreciation that there are always different meanings of things and persons. Nothing lends for only one meaning.

To view communication from the perspective of meaning is to appreciate the difference between *descriptive* language and *evaluative* language. Most communication problems have origins in our mistaking evaluative language for descriptive language. Evaluative language reflects and privileges our own values, beliefs, fears, and prejudices. Claiming that a person speaks loudly is evaluative rather than descriptive. Claiming that a person is lazy is evaluative rather than descriptive. Claiming that a person is rude is evaluative rather than descriptive. Claiming that a person is offensive is evaluative rather than descriptive. Perhaps the person you are describing as rude was merely seeking to be honest. Perhaps the person you are describing as lazy was merely tired or bored. Perhaps the person you are describing as loud was merely seeking to be heard and acknowledged. Evaluative language tends to promote hostility and resentment as the person who you are judging and characterizing is no doubt convinced that you have no right to do so. Indeed, the problem with evaluative language is that it reveals no recognition of the fact that our interpretations reflect our own subjectivity. Evaluative language is about us imposing our subjectivity on others. For again, why should the person who is merely seeking to be forthright be judged and characterized by us as being rude and offensive? How did we come to have such a right to make such a negative characterization? This is also how evaluative language undermines communication—our interpretations (our meanings) of something become an evaluation of someone and something. Ideally, our aim should be on observing and describing rather than evaluating and condemning.

Conclusion

That a Jackson Pollock painting can be valued at over a hundred million dollars makes plain that meaning ultimately resides within human beings. It also reminds us that our meaning of things is bound up with our values, our beliefs, our fears, our resources, and our experiences. Consequently, identifying or understanding another person's meaning of something can often be challenging as our own values, beliefs, fears, resources, and experiences tend to be different. From the perspective of communication as meaning, communication becomes archeology. We should be always patiently and carefully probing a person to understand what that person means. Nothing should ever be assumed. From the perspective of communication as meaning, human diversity is boundless. In being of different values, beliefs, fears, resources, and experiences, every human being is different. Again, who can fathom that a Jackson Pollock painting can be worth so much money? From the perspective of communication as meaning, communication is about understanding, yet no complete and absolute understanding of anything or any person is ever possible. Our meanings are always moving, shifting, changing, and unfolding. The best we can do is to always strive to better understand the other person's meaning of things, rather than trying to coercively impose our meaning of things on the person. In this way, our focus is always on the other. What can I do to better understand your meaning of things?

Many of our popular notions of communication are bound up with our misunderstandings of language. We continue to associate communication with being able to use language effectively, efficiently, and persuasively. We believe that acquiring such expertise involves knowing what language is supposedly offensive, and refraining from using such language. In other words, such expertise assumes that meaning resides in language. But such an assumption has no place in communication theory. *When* a word is invoked, and *how*, and *where*, and by *whom*, can fundamentally alter the meaning of a word or a phrase. This is why no poem, no song, no novel, no speech, lends for one meaning. The ambiguity found in language as a result of words always lending for different meanings means that no language can be perfectly controlled. It also makes human diversity inevitable and unconquerable.

To take diversity seriously is to recognize that all human beings, in being of different experiences, backgrounds, influences, struggles, temperaments, and resources, will always use language differently, experience language differently, and relate to language differently. As regards language and communication, nothing should ever be assumed to be one thing or another. We should *always* be probing, questioning, rephrasing, listening—in a word, communicating. To take diversity seriously is to take communication seriously. Diversity locates communication in terms of understanding. Through communication we enlarge who and what we are capable of understanding by restraining our worse instincts and impulses to shame, humiliate, and stereotype.

CHAPTER 5

DIVERSITY VERSUS INCLUSION

We refer to inclusion in terms of diversity, but how could diversity be included without being neutralized and compromised? In other words, how could diversity be included and still be diversity? Why then should diversity aspire to be included? What good does inclusion do for diversity?

We commonly assume that communication promotes inclusion. It supposedly allows us to navigate our differences and achieve common ground. It moves us from divergence to convergence, from exclusion to inclusion. However, we only believe this when we already believe that we achieve communication by vanquishing confusion. The fact is that confusion is bound up with communication. Without confusion, communication is nothing. Confusion vitalizes communication. It gives communication life and purpose. On the other hand, inclusion demands assimilation. Our diversity must be reduced to nothing that could threaten the status quo. It must be scrubbed and sanitized of everything threatening, or perceived to be so. Conformity is assumed to be necessary so that order and prosperity can prevail. *E pluribus unum*—out of many, one. Thus the metaphor of the melting pot—a certain amount of heat and cooking supposedly being necessary to make diversity inclusive and productive. Communication, however, succeeds by generating diversity, that is, by always nurturing the possibility of a different meaning, which in turn can only come from a different view of the world. Indeed, the problem of diversity is the same for communication, which is tyranny, any determination to impose one reality upon us.

To value diversity is to value communication. There can be no diversity without democracy, and no democracy without communication. Inclusion is tyranny. It is about refusing to invite and nurture different perspectives under the guise that certain views are inherently offensive and harmful. Inclusion rises by undermining communication, such as institutions and governments instituting various codes, regulations, and laws that prohibit the expressing of different views that could possibly threaten and disrupt the order of things.

At the foundation of inclusion is the belief that chaos must be subdued in order for us to have prosperity. This means managing and limiting diversity. We cannot allow it to threaten the order of things, and, in doing so, supposedly jeopardize our prosperity. It must be put in service of the status quo. We do this by first reducing diversity to four or five arbitrary categories (e.g., race, gender, sexual orientation, nationality, economic status), which really means reducing the complexity and diversity of our humanity into four or five categories. This enterprise, of course, is absurd. But notice how inclusion begins with limiting diversity. Then again, how else could diversity be included without being reduced to something that could be included? However, in limiting and distorting our diversity, inclusion limits and distorts us. It does so by undermining communication in the name of promoting civility. It stops us from doing the hard mental, emotional, existential, and spiritual work that communication demands, especially when dealing with persons fundamentally different from us. Moreover, in stopping communication, inclusion stops us from developing the practices, such as empathy and honesty, that are vital for us to become fully human—that is, from getting out of the control of our primal instincts and impulses. Ultimately, inclusion alienates us from ourselves and each other by stopping us from engaging each other directly, honestly, and compassionately.

Take the case of race. How does race promote diversity? That two persons are of the same race could barely mean anything important. Such persons could be of different religions, different backgrounds, different politics, different ambitions, different moral systems, different resources, different influences, and so forth. Race masks all of this diversity. It passes for diversity without actually promoting diversity. Yet this is how race alienates. Rather than promoting diversity, race promotes conformity by pushing us to believe that because we share the same race, we share—and should share—everything else. Thus the outrage when a member of the tribe publicly dissents with a position that supposedly represents the view of the tribe. Such diversity is never included and celebrated. There is no narrative about the person speaking truth to power. Instead, the person is normally shamed, shunned, and silenced.

Race is a creature of racism. The purpose of race was never to promote, and certainly never to celebrate, human diversity. Its purpose was always to diminish human diversity for the sake of conquest and exploitation. This is why inclusion can value, promote, and even celebrate race. Race poses no threat to anything. This is why the first Black person to occupy the White House was embraced by friends and foes for articulating an inclusion narrative that put race in the service of inclusion. (*"There is not a liberal America and a conservative America — there is the United States of America. There is not a black America and a white America and Latino America and Asian America — there's the United States of America. . . . There are no red states, no blue states, ONLY the United States of America.*") He was publicly declaring to be a threat to nothing. The status quo will remain intact. The purpose of race was always to protect the status quo, and thereby stop us from getting to a larger understanding of human oppression. Such is the problem of race. It stops us from attending to all the oppression that exceeds race, of which racism is merely one expression. We become obsessed with race. We demand that race matters. Everything must begin and end with race, meaning everything becomes racialized. We assume that the goal must be to end racism. In ending racism, all will supposedly be well. We will have inclusion and supposedly all the spoils that come with inclusion. Such again is the problem with race. In aiding and abetting inclusion, it stops us from imagining the world in new ways. It undermines liberation by making revolution impossible.

Christopher J. Lebron's (2017) new book, *The Making of Black Lives Matter: A Brief History of an Idea*, begins with an interesting admission in the introduction, "There is no doubt that the movement itself is historically momentous, even if it remains unclear as of this writing the level of policy efficacy [the Black Lives Matter movement] has been able to bring to bear on the problem of racial justice" (p. xii). Still, for Lebron, the Black Lives Matter movement is "historically momentous." It is a movement that "seeks to redeem a nation" (p. x). According Lebron, "there is something undeniably powerful about those three words: black lives matter" (p. ii). But is this really the case? That is, is this movement truly historically momentous? Did it really come to redeem a nation, and are the words "black lives matter" undeniably powerful, as Lebron claims? First, what exactly is historically momentous about the movement? In other words, what exactly distinguishes this movement from others that also sought equality and justice for Black people? Lebron never addresses any of these questions. But in what ways exactly does the Black Lives Matter movement promises to upend the status quo in ways that eluded other movements for equality and justice? In short, in what ways is the politics of the movement historically momentous? What new political strategies does the movement reflect that promise to move a people forward in ways that others were unable to? Again, Lebron never addresses these kinds of questions in any way.

Moreover, what is the intellectual disruption that makes the Black Lives Matter movement historically momentous and will help redeem a nation that certainly needs redeeming? That is, what constitutes the intellectual disruption, and one that should worry elites of power and privilege? Once again Lebron gives us no account of how the Black Lives Matter movement is intellectually superior or even different from other movements that fight for justice and equality. But what exactly constitutes, to use James Baldwin's words, the fire this time?

In addition, what is so undeniably powerful about the words "black lives matter"? As Lebron reminds us, the movement's origins and momentum can be found in the recent Black lives cut down by law enforcement. But why should only those lives cut down by law enforcement push us to contend that Black lives matter? What about all the other Black lives that are also violently cut down? Where is the outrage and mass protest over the loss of *every* Black life violently cut down? Where also is the outrage and mass protest over the mass incarceration of Black lives for nonviolent offenses? Where also is the outrage and mass protest over all the Black lives on death row, especially when most of the modern world views the death sentence as a moral abomination? How also could Black lives matter when so many Black people are fully complicit in the destruction of Black lives? Such complicity is documented in new books by James Forman (*Locking Up Our Own: Crime and Punishment in Black America*) and Michael Javen Fortner (*Black Silent Majority: The Rockefeller Drugs and the Politics of Punishment*). Where also was the outrage and mass protests as poverty was exploding under the first Black President? Does poverty have nothing to do with the condition of Black lives? Indeed, that race poses no threat to anything can be seen in Michael Eric Dyson's (2018) admission in *What Truth Sounds Like: RFK, James Baldwin, and our Unfinished Conversation about Race in America* that after two full terms in office, the first Black President was "of little practical use to black folk," doing nothing substantive or disruptive "to counter black unemployment and persistent intergenerational poverty" (pp. 211-212). He also did nothing to end the mass incarceration of black folk for nonviolent offenses.

There is nothing historically momentous about the Black Lives Matter movement. Neither does the movement possess any kind of superior political and intellectual resources to redeem a nation that continues to torment and destroy black lives. The reality is that the concept of race is a falsehood. It was always a falsehood. It was a falsehood invented by one group to justify the oppression and exploitation of another group. The fundamental problem with the Black Lives Matter movement is that it perpetuates this falsehood, and in doing so legitimizes it. The only way to end a falsehood is to expose it and release ourselves of it. But the Black Lives Matter movement has no intentions of doing either. For if we were to expose race to be a falsehood, then we would have to move on from it. We would have to find new ways of understanding over 350 years of slavery, Black Codes, and Jim Crow practices that have nothing much to do with race. The reality is that if one aspires to fully understand the misery and cruelty that human beings continue to inflict on each other in every corner of the world and in every period in history, then race is a poor device for doing so. It impedes the development of much richer and deeper understandings of the evils that human beings are capable of exacting on other human beings. So far, the Black Lives Matter movement seems to have no interest in this much larger intellectual project. It needs to hold on to race. If anything, it wants to elevate race. Race matters, and because race matters, black lives matter. However, in order to hold onto race, the black lives matter movement must hold onto a falsehood, thereby becoming bedfellows with those who invented the falsehood and continue to benefit from its perpetuation.

This is why the black lives matter movement will never pose a threat to anything. It is using the tools of the master, and as Audre Lorde eloquently told us long ago, the tools that build the house of the master will never build the house of the slave. Indeed, most damning about the black lives matter movement is the very language that names the movement. Those words that Lebron views as "undeniably powerful" indicts a community. The demand of the Black Lives Matter movement is for black lives to matter. Black lives should matter to us the way other lives matter to us. But why should lives merely matter to us? In other words, no life should merely matter to us. Instead, lives should be precious to us. The language of "matter" has no place when discussing lives, especially when the lives in question have been enslaved, brutalized, and murdered for over 350 years. Decisions matter. Choices matter. Perspectives matter. Lives, however, regardless of the color, the gender, the orientation, the status, can only be precious.

In many ways the status quo wants black lives to matter. When black lives matter, race matters, and this keeps the falsehood in place that is important to preserving the order of things. For the Black Lives Matter movement, the notion that all lives matter is offensive. Such a notion supposedly denies the reality that black lives are—and have always been—uniquely vulnerable to injustice. No doubt, such is the case. Race matters in any society that values race. However, in this society nearly all lives are disposable and exploitable. Thus the notion of black lives being uniquely vulnerable, though important, changes nothing fundamentally. What we need is a new society that stops treating all lives as disposable and exploitable.

Finally, the Black Lives Matter movement is dangerous. It legitimizes the supposed necessity of violence. I am referring to violence writ large, specifically actions and campaigns that aim to block or suppress different perspectives under the guise that certain perspectives promote hate and bigotry. Such perspectives should supposedly be suppressed by any means necessary. To condone such perspectives is supposedly to normalize them, and thus to be complicit in the supposed harm they cause. But communication is about interpretation. One person's hate speech is often something else for another person. The violence we employ against others we eventually turn upon our own. Such is also what happens when the slave uses the master's tools. Violence, rhetorical or otherwise, is a tool of the master. It is a tool of oppression, exploitation, and subjugation. As Martin Luther King Jr. and so many others knew so long ago in the civil rights movement, violence, even rhetorical violence, has no place in human affairs. It harms all in the end. No one is spared its ravages.

Conclusion

Revolutions reflect the rise of new ways of framing the world, perceiving the world, experiencing the world. Anything less than a revolution is a reaction—the slave using the master's tools to merely make alterations to the master's house. For again, what is the value of black lives mattering in a society that views most lives as disposable and exploitable? How can black lives strive in a world facing ecological peril and diminishing natural resources? Ultimately, how can black lives strive in a world that promotes so much death and destruction? This is like struggling for first class seating on the Hindenburg. No doubt, Black people should have equal access to first class seating in any setting. But why would anyone want first class on the Hindenburg? Without a new worldview there will be no new tools to build a society that views all lives as precious and thus deserving of a better world. Revolutions matter because tools matter. There can be no building of a society that finally ends human misery without the coming of a new worldview that gives us new ways of being in the world.

In the end, racism is pervasive and the world would be better off without it. But inclusion is having us mistake a symptom for cause. Racism is a symptom of a problem. It is born, as with any other kind of movement that values homogeneity, a diminished and impoverished mind. No amount of speech codes and diversity training can heal this mind. This mind can only be healed through the exercising of empathy and compassion, honesty and transparency. In short, only by pushing the mind to be more and more vulnerable is healing possible. A world without racism can never merely be a world without racism. It must also be a world without all the other kinds of human oppression. Only through our minds becoming more expansive can our worlds become so.

CHAPTER 6

INCLUSION IS AN ABSTRACTION

Institutions are made up of rules, regulations, and norms that aim to achieve order, stability, and continuity. As such, no institution can afford to promote too much diversity or (supposedly) the wrong kind of diversity and remain viable. In other words, an institution can only include, bridge, recognize, and accommodate so much diversity. In the end, any diversity must conform to the rules, regulations, and norms that constitute the institution. The case study at Syracuse University speaks compellingly to this reality. Our bridging, accommodating, and including of diversity is all about reducing diversity to something that poses no serious threat to an institution. This means reducing diversity to an abstraction—something that adds nothing of value to anything. It is diversity in name only.

What also emerges from the Syracuse University case study is that those who tend to militantly champion diversity and inclusion also tend to be violently and cruelly hostile to any diversity that is different. The only diversity that will be included, affirmed, and celebrated is that which conforms to a model of diversity that focuses on group differences rather than human differences. Any other diversity will be shamed, silenced, and banished. All of this can be seen in the following case study that is now commonly referred to as the Tuvel affair.

Tyranny in the Name of Diversity

A paper by Rebecca Tuvel, titled *In Defense of Transracialism*, was recently published in *Hypatia*, "the most widely respected journal in feminist philosophy." A firestorm then ensued that made for many headlines. All but immediately there were petitions and letters calling for the retraction of the paper, personal attacks, and threats. The author was "cautioned" that refusing to retract the paper and immediately issue a sincere apology would be "devastating . . . personally, professionally, and morally." The thesis of the paper is that "[s]ince we should accept transgender individuals' decisions to change sexes, we should also accept transracial individuals' decisions to change races." Tuvel claims that "we treat people wrongly when we block them from assuming the identity they wish to become."

Critics said that the paper constitutes "epistemic violence" and "discursive transmisogynistic violence." It also "enacts violence and perpetuates harm in numerous ways." The first petition to call for the paper to be retracted said that its "continued availability causes further harm," of which there are supposedly many caused by the paper. The petition also said that the paper "uses vocabulary and frameworks not recognized, accepted, or adopted by the conventions of the relevant subfields . . . mischaracterizes various theories and practices relating to religious identity and conversion . . . misrepresents leading accounts of belonging to a racial group . . . [and] fails to seek out and sufficiently engage with scholarly work by those who are most vulnerable to the intersection of racial and gender oppressions (women of color) in its discussion of transracialism." There was also an apology from many members of the journal's editorial board that said, "We . . . extend our profound apology to our friends and colleagues in feminist philosophy, especially transfeminists, queer feminists, and feminists of color, for the harms that the publication of the article on transracialism has caused. To compare ethically the lived experience of trans people (from a distinctly external perspective) primarily to a single example of a white person claiming to have adopted a black identity creates an equivalency that fails to recognize the history of racial appropriation, while also associating trans people with racial appropriation. We recognize and mourn that these harms will disproportionately fall upon those members of our community who continue to experience marginalization and discrimination due to racism and cisnormativity." It continued, "Clearly, the article should not have been published, and we believe that the fault for this lies in the review process. In addition to the harms listed above imposed upon trans people and people of color, publishing the article risked exposing its author to heated critique that was both predictable and justifiable. A better review process would have both anticipated the criticisms that quickly followed the publication, and required that revisions be made to improve the argument in light of those criticisms."

Then came the backlash to the backlash. In counter petitions, opinion pieces, letters to editors, and social media posts, critics of the critics made many defenses of the paper's scholarly integrity and the review process that made for its publication. The criticisms of Tuvel's paper were found to be without any kind of scholarly merit, and the notion, which was invoked again and again by critics, including Judith Butler, that the paper caused harm was described as absurd, stupid, ridiculous. Many were also appalled by how Tuvel was publicly shamed, scandalized, and threatened in the name of diversity. Below are excerpts from a few letters, articles, and counter petitions.

- *The signatories [of the first petition calling for the retraction of the paper] sent a clear message: no inquiry into the function and precepts of the prevailing philosophy of gender will be tolerated. We unequivocally reject this message and affirm our right to question, critique, and rebut any and all philosophies or viewpoints, regardless of how much academic support they may have. . . . We condemn the attempts of academics and others to silence and erase from public view an opinion solely because it does not fall within the discursive parameters that they have taken it upon themselves to set. We assert that the academics who signed on to this letter betrayed their fundamental duty as scholars to encourage — even demand — rigorous examination and robust discussion of ideas.*

- *To have signed this letter is to contribute to and be complicit in the likely destruction of the career (and therefore the life) of an untenured junior faculty member. This is a very obvious and very serious harm . . . The position that the value of preventing some possible harm to transgender people from an academic journal article that is explicitly committed to transgender rights somehow outweighs or is even equivalent to the value of protecting a highly vulnerable junior faculty member from wanton attacks on her professionalism and character stemming from the acceptance of a blind-reviewed article in a peer-reviewed journal is utterly untenable. And that doesn't even begin to address the larger question of the value of free philosophical inquiry vis-a-vis possible harm to members of an oppressed group from the publication of an academic journal article that is in fact supportive of their rights and personhood.*

- *Although it may be true that censorship from the Right is typically more overtly violent, the smug, self-righteous censorship from the Left is quite violent in its own way . . . . Some academics seemed to suggest that Tuvel made claims that went against established truths, which is just not the case. Is it an established truth that one is allowed to choose identity between male and female, but not between white and black? Far from it. And although there may be good reasons for why certain marginalized perspectives need to be respected, this does not justify dismissing a position as intellectually inferior just because you don't like it.*

- *All in all, it's remarkable how many basic facts this letter [the first petition to retract the paper] gets wrong about Tuvel's paper. Either the authors simply lied about the article's contents, or they didn't read it at all. Every single one of the hundreds of signatories on the open letter now has their name on a document that severely (and arguably maliciously) mischaracterizes the work of one of their colleagues. This is not the sort of thing that usually happens in academia — it's a really strange, disturbing instance of mass groupthink, perhaps fueled by the dynamics of online shaming and piling-on.*

- *The main charge against Tuvel is that the very existence and availability of her paper causes harm to various groups, most specifically to members of the transgender community. This is a puzzling and contentious claim that deserves serious reflection. . . . The authors of the editorial board statement have nothing to say about how they understand harm. This already should give pause for thought. Philosophers, whatever their methodological orientation or training, usually pride themselves on sensitivity to how words and concepts are used. This makes it odd to see no attention being paid to how they are understanding this key concept of harm, which is central to many areas in legal and moral philosophy.*

- *Tuvel's paper . . . is a wholly legitimate, if provocative, philosophical endeavor. One can agree or disagree, or wish the author had done more of this or less of that. But the assertion that broaching the very subject produces inevitable harm is specious, to say the least. Indeed, the idea that any article in a specialized feminist journal causes harm, and even violence, as the signatories to an ope*n letter to the journal claim, is a grave misuse of the term "harm."

Let us note the many abstractions that appear in the criticisms of Tuvel's paper, beginning with transgenderism, transracialism, transfeminists, queer feminists, and feminists of color. We are to assume that human beings belong first and foremost to groups, and that homogeneity rather than diversity is what unites and binds members of a group. Our groups supposedly define how we make sense of ourselves, and also how we perceive and experience the world. Our groupings are us. We are groups. In offending groups, human beings are being offended as supposedly all members of any group are of the same sensibility, rationality, modality, spirituality, and so forth. Supposedly, our diversity resides in our membership in different groupings, thus protecting our diversity is about protecting and preserving the integrity of our groupings. Any attack on our groupings is supposedly an attack on us.

However, because our common groupings are nothing but abstractions, meaning that members have never once met to decide, declare, and pledge allegiance to a common set of values, beliefs, ambitions, and principles, any perceived attack on any group that supposedly causes harm has to be announced by a select few with the power and means to do so. This means a select few invoking a tremendous level of egotism and narcissism. Rather than declaring that "I find Tuvel's paper to be offensive," I now declare that "Tuvel's paper is offensive to transfeminists, queer feminists, and feminists of color," without ever polling members of these groups or even getting any kind of permission to speak on behalf of all members of these groups. This is why Tuvel's critics can use the notion of harm so recklessly, twisting and distorting it "beyond all recognition" (Bermudez, 2017, Walters, 2017). Tuvel's critics are viewing diversity from the level of abstract groupings rather than the level of living human beings who struggle everyday to make sense of life and the human experience. This is also why Tuvel's critics have such a shallow view of human diversity. Tuvel's critics want nothing to do with our complexity, and everything that makes for our complexity. For when is the queer feminist no longer a daughter, or a sister, or an aunt, or a grandmother, or a friend, or a neighbor, or a teacher, or a wife, or a cousin, a soccer coach, a member of the school board, a pacifist, an environmentalist, a cellist in a local orchestra? How does any grouping begin to account for all this complexity? In the end, no amount of groupings can begin to capture our diversity in all its infinite forms and expressions. We each have our own diversity, reflecting our different experiences, circumstances, resources, privileges, struggles, and influences, and should be allowed to live our lives on our own terms and conditions. Without liberty, diversity is nothing. In the words of Justice Anthony Kennedy, "At the heart of liberty is the right to define one's own concept of existence, of meaning, of the universe, and of the mystery of human life."

Diversity means that each person is of different narrative, and no person should ever assume to know the full topography of our narrative. To insist, either openly or insidiously, that one person's narrative conforms to the standards, expectations, and ambitions found in another person's narrative is nothing but tyranny. In fact, besides the reckless invoking of harm, what is also disturbing about the Tuvel affair is the hostility to human diversity. For why should any of us have to seek the blessing of the leadership of any abstract group in order to live our lives on our own terms and conditions? Why should any person be compelled in this way? Case in point, Tina Fernandes Botts, a philosophy professor, said that a major problem with Tuvel's paper is that she misses the difference between race and gender (even though Tuvel explicitly says in the paper, "My thesis relies in no way upon the claim that race and sex are equivalent, or historically constructed in exactly the same way"). Unlike gender, race is supposedly a function of ancestry, and thus only someone with black ancestors can count as black. Cressida Heyes, who also called for the retraction of Tuvel's paper, claims that society's beliefs about what race *is* limits race change. As such, "the belief that an individual's racial identity derives from her biological ancestors undermines the possibility of changing race, in ways that contrast with sex-gender." But as Tuvel perceptively notes, "to say this is how racial categorization currently operates in our society is to provide a very poor reason to the person asking how racial categorization should operate," which "makes it difficult to see how we can make any social progress at all." In fact, why should any person be compelled in any way to abide by our society's biological beliefs about race, especially a society with a history of over 350 years of slavery, Black codes, and Jim Crow practices that was all based on a biological view of race? When did this society ever do well by race to now have the moral authority to control what others do with race? Moreover, what of the claim that race is nothing but a creature of racism? How does the rigid preserving of race contribute to the making of a world without racism? What also of Audre Lorde's axiom that the tools of the master—in this case a biological view of race—will never build the house of the slave? Moreover, why should any person be compelled to abide by Botts' and Heyes' conception of race and racial belonging, or else face threats and vitriol? Who made any person the new race police with the moral authority to socially and professionally punish any human being who wishes to embody race in ways that pose no kind of physical or material harm to others? Why should this kind of policing be permitted, and how exactly does it promote rather than undermine human diversity?

Finally, what of all the cruelty found in the personal attacks on Tuvel? What does such cruelty reveal about the value and purchase of higher education in terms of helping us navigate our differences? It is now generally agreed that nothing was fundamentally wrong with Tuvel's paper. There was no plagiarism, no fabrication of data, no intent in any way to harm or hurt any person. The calls for retraction were purely about erasing and silencing a perspective that was different. That Tuvel's paper was judged to have flaws was merely a pretext for the shaming, threatening, and silencing. There would simply be no inclusion of Tuvel's perspective. It had to be silenced and erased for the sake of preserving the status quo in feminist philosophy. The cruelty that Tuvel met reflects our lack of empathy and compassion for any diversity that is outside of our model of diversity. It reflects our narcissism. This is why there was no regard for what the calls for retraction would do to Tuvel's life and career. Instead, the concern was for abstract groupings that had nothing to do with anything. This was the pretext for the narcissism. This is why cruelty is the hallmark of narcissism, and pervades inclusion and diversity issues. It is also why Syracuse University had no qualms handing down sentences that would egregiously harm the futures of so many students, and why no faculty or department issued any statement condemning the lack of empathy and compassion.

Undermining Abstractions

Abstractions distance and separate us from what is real. Such is the nature of inclusion. It is nothing but an abstraction. It has no foundation in anything real. It is purely a creature of ideology, meaning a creature of a certain set of beliefs, values, and fears. Race, gender, nationality, sexual orientation, and other such identity markers are all abstractions that aim to suppress human diversity. Again, when ten persons claim to be of the same race, what does that mean in terms of our understanding the humanity and diversity of these people? Why must we assume that race can account for a proper description of these ten people? Why must these ten people be defined and experienced by their supposed homogeneity rather than their diversity? What is the irony of using homogeneity to promote diversity?

We assume that being of the same race means the same thing for all ten persons. We speak of people being of the same culture, thereby assuming that homogeneity defines a human ecology. But this, of course, is false. Yet we continue to insist that these kinds of abstractions—like culture, race, gender, nationality, and so forth—matter in terms of defining and capturing our diversity. We also insist that we continue to use these abstractions to define ourselves and guide how we relate to others. However, abstractions like race, gender, nationality, and sexual orientation obliterate human diversity by flattening out our differences. For instance, as much as I am of a certain race on paper, how I define and experience my being might have nothing to do with race. So whereas being of a certain race could mean something to one person, it could also mean nothing to another. It is, after all, an abstraction. It is something we put in the world rather than something we find in the world.

Life will go on without race. The universe will go on without race. Race contributes nothing to the betterment of the universe. It is purely a creature of racism. Why then do we continue to value race? Why do we continue to claim that race—like gender, nationality, and sexual orientation—should matter in terms of appreciating our diversity when the purpose of these notions was always to diminish human diversity? There is simply no way that our common groupings of human diversity can begin to reflect our diversity, complexity, and hybridity. But this is how abstractions separate and distance from what is real.

Conclusion

Abstractions undermine communication by engendering division, separation, and fragmentation. For when I declare, for example, that I am heterosexual and you declare that you are homosexual, we are both assuming that in (supposedly) being different, there is division and separation between us. Your issues are supposedly different to mine, and we would supposedly do well to bridge, accommodate, and include our differences. Our different sexual orientations supposedly constitute our differences. We also assume that our communication should acknowledge these differences. In fact, we insist that communication preserve and elevate our abstractions, such as insisting that we follow all the rules laid down by the race police, the gender police, and sexual orientation police. However, in doing so, communication only succeeds in preserving our illusions and delusions. What then can communication make possible when we insist that communication sustains our illusions and delusions? That is, how can communication threaten the status quo when we insist that it first sustains the status quo? Put another way, how can communication attend to difference when we insist that communication diminish difference?

Attending to difference means recognizing that each person is different as a result of different experiences, different tribulations, different resources, different influences, different circumstances, and so forth. All of these differences make for different meanings, different understandings, different modes of being. Communication is about attending to our differences, that is, our different ways of interpreting and experiencing the world that in turn reflect our different ways of being in the world with others. This is how communication threatens the status quo, by recognizing and elevating human diversity in all its boundless expressions. Conversely, abstractions diminish communication by blocking communication from emancipating diversity. All that remains is the illusion of diversity. If human diversity is to flourish, communication must flourish. Communication thrives by promoting diversity.

Abstractions also undercut communication by removing the intensity and even the ferocity that come with human diversity. Human diversity means tension, conflict, and disagreement.

Human diversity means that we value different things. What can be important to one person can mean nothing to another. Human diversity also means that what I find to be appropriate can be different from what you find to be so. We can react differently to the same thing. Of course nothing is inherently wrong with tension, conflict, and disagreement. But because we continue to be in age of abstractions, an age hostile to human diversity, we insist that there be no tension, no conflict, no disagreement, or at least any that is intense and genuine. No person must be offended. Our own entitled sensibility must be privileged. There must be no contesting or even denouncing of our sensibility. We even demand our sensibility be institutionally protected through speech codes and other practices prohibiting persons from unsettling our sensibility. Communication must be tamed, sanitized, and civilized. In a word, communication must be depoliticized, stripped of any power to threaten anything. This means stripping us of the power to disrupt anything. So rather than being honest, we must for the (supposed) sake of civility, collegiality, and diversity, be disingenuous. We must say that your position is interesting when in fact we find it to be ridiculous. In order to protect your entitled sensibility we must save you from human diversity, which we accomplish by reducing communication to nothing. For again, without promoting and cultivating human diversity in all its expressions, communication becomes nothing, devoid of any power to threaten the status quo.

However, what ultimately becomes of the quality of the human experience when communication is tamed, sanitized, and neutralized? How do we acquire the resilience, fortitude, and forbearance to strive in a world where human diversity is everywhere? How do we become democratic and pluralistic when communication becomes nothing? In other words, without being comfortable with tension, conflict, and disagreement, how does democracy become possible and robust? We become nothing when communication becomes nothing. For without communication, diversity becomes impossible. What now passes for diversity are nothing but abstractions of diversity.

Finally, abstractions foster human misery by promoting and sustaining alienation. Alienation disfigures our view of things by making us afraid of ourselves and each other. It makes for a worldview that is laden with fear and anxiety. Alienation also dehumanizes us. In separating us from ourselves, alienation robs us of the power to act boldly and imaginatively. It makes us cowardly. Moreover, alienation fosters cruelty by undermining empathy and compassion. In separating us from ourselves, alienation separates us from all the struggles that come with the human experience. This is how alienation makes for a false consciousness. It releases us from what is real, what is important. Yet such is also the seduction of alienation. It allows us to live in a world of abstractions, a world that wants nothing to do with what is real. In promoting and circulating all kinds of abstractions, alienation makes us reckless by masking the fact that all our actions and decisions have consequences and implications, and these consequences and implications always fall back on us.

CHAPTER 7
INCLUSION DELUSIONS

Syracuse University did what nearly every other university does after a supposed diversity incident blows up and causes embarrassment. It immediately promised to do a list of things to promote diversity and inclusion:

1. make new diversity faculty hires and devote more resources to attracting and retaining minority students,

2. allocate more resources to support diversity and inclusion initiatives so as to make the university more safe for diverse students, faculty, and staff,

3. mandate more diversity training with sessions on "the value of variety and building a culture of inclusion and diversity, identifying barriers and overcoming difficulties in communications when cultural understandings vary, and setting individual examples and developing further educational opportunities regarding diversity and inclusion,"

4. create new diversity and inclusion administrative departments (Office of Inclusive Excellence) and positions

(Assistant Dean for Inclusive Excellence) in every school across the university to monitor and implement diversity and inclusion policy,

5. increase the number of course offerings that promote diversity and inclusion,

6. create another new administrative position (Chief Diversity Officer) that will report directly to the Chancellor and "play a critical role in our ongoing efforts to identify and propose solutions to ensure a more diverse, inclusive and welcoming environment for students, faculty, staff and visitors,"

7. hire an outside diversity consultant to advise senior administrators and conduct training across the university,

8. require an expanded section on every syllabus that addresses diversity and inclusion,

9. institute Indigenous Peoples Day as a campus initiative to honor indigenous history and culture on the second Monday of October,

10. create a shared reading and discussion experience with small groups of new students focused on topics including identity, inclusion, and belonging,

11. appoint a new Provost Faculty Fellow who will implement a professional development program to assist faculty in fostering a more culturally inclusive classroom,

12. appoint a new Graduate Dean Faculty Fellow for Diversity and Inclusion, who will be responsible for promoting the Graduate School's diversity and inclusion goals,

13. develop a Strategic Inclusive Excellence Program that "uses dialogue to develop inclusive excellence leadership skills,"

14. create a new Inclusive Excellence Council in the College of Engineering and Computer Science,

15. create a new mandatory diversity and inclusion course for all undergraduates, beginning Fall 2019, and

16. create new "inclusive teaching workshops" for faculty "to enhance self-awareness, detect and respond to unconscious bias, and strengthen their skills for more inclusive classrooms, labs, studios, and field experiences." According to Martha Diede, director of the University's new Center for Teaching and Learning Excellence, "these workshops are the beginning of a concerted effort on the part of the University community to become more inclusive. As inclusion professionals will tell you—the work of inclusion is never fully completed."

The consultant that Syracuse University hired was Damon A. Williams, the leader of the National Inclusive Excellence Leadership Academy and "a national expert on diversity and inclusion." Williams supposedly has worked with over 1,000 colleges and universities and was described as a "visionary and inspirational leader." He recently launched "The Inclusive Excellence Tour" that offers "a chance to strengthen your organization's diversity commitment by engaging your entire community in a conversation about diversity, equity, inclusion, and change with Dr. Damon A. Williams." The tour includes a "working session . . . that is specifically designed to motivate and empower chief, senior, and campus diversity officers, diversity groups, . . . multicultural marketing officers, and diversity and inclusion champions across all roles and levels of the community." It also includes an "executive coaching session . . . that is uniquely designed to help your CEO or president hack the diversity, equity, and inclusion challenges impeding progress in your organization," and a "private book signing with the author [Williams] of the only diversity and inclusion strategy books endorsed by the presidents of the American Educational Research Association (AERA), American Council of Education (ACE), Association of Americans Colleges and Universities (AACU), National Association of Student Administrators (NASPA), National Collegiate Athletics Association (NCAA), and the National Association of College and University Business Officers (NACUBO)." Damon Williams came on the heels of another diversity and inclusion specialist, Kathy Obear, who Syracuse University hired to host "a three-day retreat focused on diversity and inclusion" for the Chancellor, vice chancellors, and other university leaders. Out of the retreat a workgroup was created to "develop solutions on how to further create a more diverse and inclusive climate."

As with nearly every other university, Syracuse University is assuming that inclusion is achieved by adding and supporting diversity. Supposedly, the university will be better off by bridging, accommodating, and including diversity. Inclusion supposedly saves us from the ravages of chaos, disunity, and conflict. It represents cooperation and collaboration, stability and continuity, peace and prosperity. In a statement to the university community, the new Chief Diversity Officer at Syracuse University said that "Positive coexistence happens when each person feels deeply welcomed and appreciated. We value diverse identities." However, no institution can afford to welcome and appreciate every kind of diverse identity. As such, how does Syracuse University plan to identify which diverse identities will be welcomed and appreciated? The new Chief Diversity Officer never broaches this matter. We are only told that

"The lived experiences of every member of Syracuse University shall be respected and embraced." But this is highly disingenuous as the university has no intention of respecting and embracing those members who wish to engage in consensual personal relationships with other members of Syracuse University. Neither does the university plan to welcome and embrace members who, on religious grounds, view homosexuality as a moral abomination. In fact, the university has no intention of "deeply" welcoming and embracing many kinds of diverse identities. The reality is that an institution can only promote so much diversity and only of the kind that poses no threat to its stability and continuity. In the end, order must rule, and order demands conformity. So what passes for the promotion and inclusion of diversity is really the pacification and assimilation of diversity. One way that institutions limit diversity is through rules, regulations, and norms that demand conformity by all, regardless of differences. Another way is by limiting ambiguity, which in turn limits communication. Ambiguity is the lifeblood of communication. It vitalizes communication. Without ambiguity, meaning is impossible. Diversity is about different things meaning different things to different peoples. So when meaning is stifled, diversity is impossible. Finally, institutions limit diversity by reducing diversity to plurality, and then passing off plurality as diversity.

Plurality is about addition, accommodation, and inclusion. It assumes that our differences reside within our groupings. It is about adding members from different groups and then having members of these groups abide by a common set of rules, standards, and norms, such as refraining from using certain kinds of language, and agreeing to be tolerant of each other's differences. Plurality is diversity in name only. Diversity, on the other hand, is about disruption, confrontation, and revolution. It poses a threat to the order of things by pushing us to promote—rather than merely accommodate, tolerate, and bridge—new ways of being that affirm life. Promoting diversity involves, among other things, dismantling structures and arrangements that block such processes, as well as promoting environs and practices that encourage new modes of being. Diversity is about possibility and the forces that promote possibility. However, when diversity becomes plurality, this force goes away. So even though institutions may come to have increasing numbers of historically marginalized and disenfranchised persons, and thereby claim diversity, such additions can also potentially work to mask our own complicity in promoting a status quo that is hostile to diversity. Plurality constitutes the most insidious threat to diversity by promoting and reifying the belief that inclusion is possible without disruption, confrontation, and revolution. However, inclusion outside of disruption, confrontation, and revolution is nothing.

Plurality pervades academe. In academe it has found its most fertile conditions upon which to thrive. Merely look at the job descriptions for positions in academe and you will find it doing what it aims to do—pretending to convince us that the institution values diversity when in reality it wants nothing to do with diversity. In every job description there is the mandatory section about how the institution values diversity and how minority peoples are "especially" encouraged to apply. In many ways these sections now function as public relations, showcasing how genuinely the institution supposedly cares about diversity and inclusion.

Job descriptions for communication positions reveal much about how plurality masquerades as diversity. In these job descriptions, diversity is understood as difference, as access to people from other worlds who differ from others in terms of race, ethnicity, ability, and/or sexuality (e.g., "We are committed to ethnic, racial, and gender diversity in our faculty and strongly encourage applications from members of underrepresented groups. We encourage applications from individuals who demonstrate a commitment to social justice, diversity, and the inclusion of all persons in serving both undergraduate and graduate students from diverse racial, ethnic, and gender groups"). Diversity is reduced to physical rather than epistemological (theoretical, conceptual, and methodological) differences. By adding, meaning including, other folks, diversity will supposedly be achieved and all will be well. However, even though the institution seeks diversity, every applicant must fit with the epistemology that guides the department in terms of theory, methodology, and pedagogy. Case in point, most job positions that include caveats for diversity, equality, affirmative action, and so on, seek only candidates whose scholarly and teaching interests align with the status quo of the respective programs. There is no apparent recognition that no epistemology can ever be separated from a worldview. Indeed, to privilege a certain epistemology is to privilege a certain worldview. Thus, to demand that other peoples uphold a certain epistemological perspective or suffer punitively, such as being deprived tenure-track positions and careers at schools with abundant resources, undermines any possibility of diversity and inclusion.

Consider the specifications for the following five positions that come with the mandatory sections about seeking diversity:

> The Department of Communication Studies at the University of Georgia seeks to fill a tenure-track faculty position of Interpersonal Communication with secondary interest in Health Communication at the rank of Assistant Professor. The successful candidate will teach large lecture undergraduate courses in interpersonal communication, quantitative research methods . . . as well as courses in communication theory . . . . At the graduate level, successful candidates will teach seminars in communication theory, quantitative research methods, health communication, and topics related to his or her research. . . . The

Franklin College of Arts and Sciences, its many units, and the University of Georgia are committed to increasing the diversity of its faculty and students, and sustaining a work and learning environment that is inclusive. Women, minorities and people with disabilities are strongly encouraged to apply. The University is an EEO/AA institution.

⋘⋙

The School of Communication at The Ohio State University invites applicants for an open rank position in the area of political communication with an emphasis on mass communication, interpersonal communication, communication technology, or some combination of the three. The School is committed to empirical, social-scientific research on communication processes, either basic or applied, making original and substantively important contributions, and is regularly ranked among the top communication research programs in the country. We seek colleagues who will help us continue this tradition and can envision research projects and courses that will be attractive to graduate and undergraduate students from within the major, and speak to the interests and needs of non-majors.

⋘⋙

The Department of Communication Arts at the University of Wisconsin-Madison seeks a social scientist for a tenured or tenure-track faculty position in Communication Science. Candidates with a Ph. D. in Communication or an affiliated social science discipline will be considered. A successful candidate must demonstrate strong quantitative methodological competency and conduct research via social scientific methods in any of the areas pertinent to interpersonal communication and social influences, including (but not limited to) interpersonal relationships, family communication, interpersonal influence, message production, persuasion, nonverbal communication, and social networks. Candidates should be able to teach courses at the undergraduate and graduate levels, and develop and/or maintain a productive research program appropriate to a major public research university.

⚬⚬⚬

The Department of Communication Arts and Sciences at The Pennsylvania State University seeks a tenure-track assistant or associate professor whose research advances communication theory, demonstrates a sophisticated command of quantitative methods, and provides insight into socially relevant problems.

⚬⚬⚬

The Department of Communication at Michigan State University seeks applicants for two tenure-track positions at the Assistant Professor level. We are seeking faculty to teach and conduct research in (1) specialties combining social influence, persuasive communication, sales communication, social marketing, health campaigns, interpersonal communication or leadership; (2) international and intercultural communication, particularly related to health and risk communication. Qualified applicants should have a social scientific focus, a background in quantitative research methods, and expertise to teach both graduate and undergraduate courses. We are seeking candidates with strong potential for a successful career in grant-supported research and who will provide mentorship for graduate students. Minority candidates are especially encouraged to apply. MSU is an Affirmative Action/Equal Opportunity Institution.

⌘

The University of Michigan Department of Communication Studies seeks applicants for two tenure track/tenured positions.

Position One: A quantitative social scientist with a strong preference for a senior scholar in media psychology, who studies the societal and individual effects of traditional and/or emerging media and whose methods include experiments, surveys, longitudinal studies, content analysis, meta analysis, and other social science techniques. While all areas of emphasis will be considered, areas of particular interest are the psychological antecedents and consequences of media use; representations of gender in the media; media effects on children and young people; media effects on health behavior; media effects on sexuality, sexual orientation and sexual attitudes; representations of race and/or ethnicity in the media; media effects on racial identity and attitudes; and media effects on cognitive processing and learning.

Position Two: A social scientist, who studies the societal and individual effects of traditional and/or emerging media and whose methods include experiments, surveys, quantitative content analysis and other social science techniques. Areas of particular interest are the effects of media on politics and public policy or on political attitudes; the news media and politics; public opinion and civic engagement; the interplay between polls, politicians and the media; the effects of partisan media; media priming and framing; processes leading to patterns of political communication, as well as the effects of these processes; the media and political socialization; political advertising; the effects of political communication on attitudes towards race, gender and class; media and voter behavior; and new media and political behavior.

These communication departments have no interest in diversity. Plurality is being passed off as diversity. There is no interest in persons of different epistemological stances, such as the person who brings a narrative focus, or a postcolonial focus, or an indigenous focus to the study of communication. As such, what becomes of those outstanding persons with tremendous records of scholarly accomplishment, and even of minority racial status, who bring fundamentally different epistemological and pedagogical perspectives to the study of the advertised areas? Evidently, such perspectives, meaning such diversity, will neither be included nor accommodated in these departments. Indeed, what is most striking about these ads is the unwillingness of these departments to even consider other possible ways of studying and theorizing about the advertised communication areas.

Ironically, this ideological and epistemological disciplining that goes on in many of the most prominent communication departments in the US is also found in many advertisements for intercultural communication positions, such as the following:

We are seeking faculty to teach and conduct research in International and Intercultural communication, particularly related to health and risk communication. Qualified applicants should have a social science focus, a background in quantitative research methods, and expertise to teach both graduate and undergraduate courses. We are seeking candidates with strong potential for a successful career in grant-supported research and who will provide mentorship for graduate students.

❦

Assistant or Associate Professor in Intercultural Communication. The successful candidate will have expertise in quantitative approaches to intercultural communication. In addition, the successful candidate will have the ability to teach quantitative research methods, statistical analysis, and/or mathematical modeling of communication processes.

❦

Assistant Professor in Intercultural Communication. The successful candidate will be able to teach and engage in research in persuasion and social influence from a cognitive approach (e.g., negotiation and conflict management, political communication, message design and production, compliance gaining) or in intercultural communication. The successful candidate will have the ability to teach quantitative research methods, statistical analysis, and/or mathematical modeling of communication processes.

These intercultural communication job descriptions show well the insidious role that job descriptions play in suppressing diversity in communication departments. These jobs ads are all written in ways that limit the scholarship that can potentially occur in these departments by requiring applicants to adhere to an epistemological stance as dictated by the department. With these ads there is simply no opportunity for persons with differing worldviews to present a different way of understanding these areas. These departments have already determined what kind of epistemology is acceptable and the worldviews to which students in these departments will be introduced. By imposing a certain epistemology on all applicants, these departments are also dictating which human practices will be conceptualized and theorized, such as how communication will be defined and theorized.

One would guess that intercultural communication positions, of all the subfields in communication studies, would allow for the most epistemological and pedagogical flexibility, as intercultural communication should at least begin with the premise that the world is rich with peoples who hold different views, including different systems of understanding, experiencing, and framing the world. Accordingly, the study of these peoples may most likely involve epistemologies that are different from those in the mainstream of communication studies. Thus, any commitment to understand the world's many different peoples must at least reflect an openness to any epistemology that is most amenable to the understanding of different peoples. In this regard, intercultural communication should demand the most epistemological diversity. It is also hurt the most by the lack of such diversity. In fact, when communication departments and schools undercut diversity by insisting on only recruiting persons of a certain epistemological orientation, these departments and schools undercut the mission of communication studies to introduce students from diverse backgrounds to a variety of epistemologies necessary to understand different peoples, and to be a discipline that welcomes peoples from all corners of the world who come to the study of communication from different epistemological orientations.

Textbooks and Inclusion

However, job advertisements are by no means the only places where communication studies disguises plurality as diversity. Nearly all of the most popular intercultural communication textbooks also engage in this disguising by perpetuating many questionable assumptions. What emerges is an intercultural communication theory and pedagogy that lacks the rigor and sophistication to deal generously with the increasing diversity and complexity that the world is imposing on us as our spaces and distances collapse and implode.

Textbooks are important books and succeed by appearing to be ideologically and epistemologically neutral. However, no book, even a textbook, is devoid of human subjectivity. Every textbook reflects a vision of how the world is and how the world should be. Also, every textbook, by reinforcing and promoting a vision of the world, reinforces various structures and arrangements of power and privilege that are complementary to such a vision of the world. Suffice it to say, textbooks play an important role in preserving the order of things.

Any list of the most popular intercultural communication textbooks would include, Hall's *Among Cultures;* Gudykunst's *Crosscultural and Intercultural Communication;* Gudykunst and Kim's *Communication with Strangers;* Weaver's *Culture, Communication and Conflict;* Rogers and Steinfatt's *Intercultural Communication;* Gudykunst's *Theorizing about Intercultural Communication;* Cooper, Calloway-Thomas, and Simonds' *Intercultural Communication;* Klopf and McCroskey's *Intercultural Communication Encounters;* Martin and Nakayama's *Intercultural Communication in Contexts;* Neuliep's *Intercultural Communication;* and Samovar, Porter, and McDaniel's *Intercultural Communication,* and *Communication Between Cultures.* All of these textbooks share many common themes and assumptions. All begin with the assumption that cultures are different in such ways as peoples' sharing different beliefs, values, fears, norms, expectations, truths, and, ultimately, different behaviors. Klopf and McCroskey (2007) contend that "Unless we know the rules of other cultures' practices, we will discover it is almost impossible to tell how members of other cultures will behave in similar situations" (p. 22). Many of these intercultural communication textbooks focus on how peoples are different as a result of being of different cultures that are either collectivist or individualist, monochromic or polychromic, high context or low context, active or passive, vertical or horizontal, universalist or particularist, masculine or feminine, instrumental or expressive, associative or abstractive, and so forth. In other words, all of these textbooks assume that diversity resides in group differences. To know our group differences is supposedly to know and understand our diversity.

These intercultural communication textbooks also cast communication as a tool that allows us to navigate and bridge our cultural differences. We will supposedly become communicatively proficient by knowing how cultures are different and how best to use various communication skills and techniques to navigate and bridge such differences. McDaniel, Samovar, and Porter (2006) claim that "The international community is riven with sectarian violence arising from ideological, cultural, and racial differences" (p. 15). Neuliep (2000) echoes Arthur Schlesinger's warning that "history tells an ugly story of what happens when people of diverse cultural, ethnic, religious, or linguistic backgrounds converge in one place" (p. 2). Finally, many intercultural communication textbooks highlight how global demographics and international business practices are demanding that every person be now interculturally proficient. According to Rogers and Steinfatt (1999), "If individuals could attain a higher degree of intercultural competence, they would presumably become better citizens, students, teachers, businesspeople, and so forth. Society would be more peaceful, more productive, and generally a more attractive place to live" (p. 222). Moreover, "Individuals would be better able to understand others who are unlike themselves. Through such improved understanding, a great deal of conflict could be avoided; the world would be a better place" (p. 222). In short, in nearly all of these textbooks, the focus is on discourses of plurality that encourage toleration and accommodation. Such a thread also persists in many discussions of language.

Nearly all of the popular intercultural communication textbooks view language as foundational to communication. The most common assumption is that a common language is vital for communication between peoples of different cultures. Thus for Samovar, Porter, and McDaniel (2007), "language diversity presents a problem in the United States" (p. 182). Although Samovar et al. "do not endorse" legislative "proposals to make English the official language of the United States," they do believe "that knowledge of English and the ability to communicate in English are essential in American society" (pp. 182-183). However, the position that "language diversity presents a problem in the United States" still perpetuates the assumption that diversity needs to be carefully managed so as to avoid chaos and social devolution. This position is no way fundamentally different to that found in the English-only movement and other initiatives to limit language diversity in the US. It merely constitutes a gentler and milder version—one that seems progressive and even supportive of diversity, yet still perpetuates the belief that inclusion demands the lessening of our differences.

Indeed, none of the intercultural communication textbooks makes any mention of the fact that history makes no case that language diversity threatens stability and social evolution. Nearly all of the world's most horrendous crimes occurred in places—such as Germany, Yugoslavia, Rwanda, Iraq, Turkey, and Somalia—that actually had a common language. Moreover, in focusing on issues, such as language diversity, that *really* pose no threat to the ability of different peoples to find harmony and understanding, many intercultural communication texts are able to side step other issues that do threaten harmony and understanding. Case in point, what of the widening gap between rich and poor, or our reckless and self-ish plundering of the planet's natural resources? How did these and other such issues come to present no problem to intercultural relations in the United States, and hence come to be absent from all of the most popular intercultural communication textbooks? Indeed, the disguising of plurality as diversity can be seen in the omission of any discussion of poverty and inequality in most inter-cultural communication textbooks.

Nearly all intercultural communication textbooks focus on teaching us how best to navigate, negotiate, and bridge group differences. The assumption is that group differences ultimately result in strife and conflict. Group differences are cast as a set of dangerous and peril-ous rapids that demand vigilant and sensitive navigation. Any wrong act, movement, behavior, or word can supposedly send us crashing into the rocks and currents of discord. But an ecological perspec-tive moves us away from this popular intercultural approach by cast-ing diversity as a verb rather than a noun, and thereby reminding us that only communication ends aggression. This perspective brings into view the many tensions, conflicts, and disagreements that are found among supposedly homogenous peoples. Yet our differences pose no inevitable threat to discord and conflict. Our supposedly intercultural problems are really ecological problems—problems that stem from the undermining of evolution. Put differently, our supposed diversity problems are fundamentally ecological in ori-gin, reflecting a lack of permeability, diversity, embeddedness, and harmony in our social, cultural, and communicational processes. No amount of sensitivity or respect for one another's differences can save us from the anguish that will come from systems that dis-rupt learning and innovation. Any system that promotes hostility to that which is different, complex, and unknown will always pro-duce strife and discord. In this way, such systems, and the differ-ences that come from these systems, should neither be tolerated nor accommodated. To look at human systems ecologically is to look at diversity in terms of evolution, with evolution implying disruption, confrontation, and even revolution. It is about promoting emergent models of communication that can push us to evolve, innovate, and change, rather than merely accommodate, tolerate, and bridge. Only evolution, and models of communication that promote evolution, will ultimately save us from ourselves and one another.

Yet intercultural communication textbooks remain focused on language. Neuliep (2000) asserts, "Intercultural communication occurs whenever a minimum of two persons from different cultures or microcultures come together and exchange verbal and nonverbal symbols" (p. 18). Likewise, Klopf and McCroskey (2007) hold that "communication is the process by which persons share information, meaning, and feelings through the exchange of verbal and nonverbal messages" (p. 34). For Samovar, Porter, and McDaniel (2007), "communication is the process through which symbols are transmitted for the purpose of eliciting a response" (p. 12). Indeed, most intercultural communication textbooks forward definitions of communication that assume no profound relationship between communication and the human condition, or even between communication and the condition of the world. Communication is cast as a tool to share our thoughts and emotions, and communication competency is about mastery of various skills and techniques. But this orientation masks the implications of different communication practices on the human condition. To recognize the profound relationship between communication and the human condition is to recognize that communication is fundamentally a moral enterprise—our communication practices and environs shape and define our humanity and the humanity of others, and the condition of our humanity affects the condition of the world. Communication is both a human-making and world-making activity.

Just from looking at communication job announcements and intercultural communication textbooks, what seems plain is that many communication departments remain off limits to many of us for the only reason that our worldviews are different, and thereby our ways of understanding communication are different. Even many intercultural communication announcements provide no opportunity for the presentation of a different story of communication for consideration. The rigid epistemological guidelines of many job announcements at the most prestigious communication departments in the US allow for no communication among peoples of different worldviews. This is the interesting irony about the lack of diversity in communication studies—the undermining of communication between different peoples by persons who are supposedly committed to the study and promotion of communication. Yet this irony reminds us why communication is integral to the promotion of diversity. Communication sustains the possibility of diversity and most distinguishes diversity from plurality. Communication puts our differences in communion with one another. It allows us to demystify the different forces that make us human, and to reckon with these forces.

Conclusion

The struggle for diversity has long been cast as a struggle for space—specifically for spaces that will shelter and nourish the best ambitions of historically marginalized and disenfranchised peoples. In this regard, the struggle has always been about inclusion. But inclusion depoliticizes diversity. Analysis of job announcements in communication studies shows that many who are already marginalized and disenfranchised will remain marginalized and disenfranchised as inclusion demands submission, meaning our promise to aid and abet no forces that might disrupt the status quo. Unfortunately, this promise often translates to historically marginalized and disenfranchised peoples being complicit in perpetuating the illusion of separation between communication theory and intercultural communication theory, and thereby perpetuating the false belief that certain understandings of communication have nothing to do with culture and history.

All communication is cultural. That there is communication theory and intercultural communication theory is an illusion that in no way serves the promotion of diversity in communication studies. Still, upholding this illusion is foundational to maintaining the status quo in communication studies, including keeping historically marginalized and disenfranchised peoples confined to jobs, convention panels, journals, and anthologies that focus upon intercultural communication and other matters that supposedly deal *only* with race, culture, ethnicity, and sexuality. The impression that emerges is that communication theory is devoid of race, culture, and privilege, and thereby beyond the limitations of human subjectivity. It is supposedly outside of history and culture, and, consequently, superior to intercultural communication theory. But no theory is ever outside of time and space, history and culture. Every theory describes as well as reinforces a vision of the world. Still, in maintaining the illusion between communication theory and intercultural communication theory, which means supporting intercultural communication initiatives so that historically marginalized and disenfranchised peoples can claim to have a space in communication studies, and thus feel included and accommodated, the status quo in communication studies wins.

Inclusion blocks any rigorous scrutiny of the dominant worldview that rules communication theory, inquiry, and pedagogy, and thereby the jobs and textbooks that help maintain this hegemony. The paradigm of inclusion, toleration, and accommodation needs to be displaced by a paradigm of evolution, innovation, and confrontation. Without this displacement, the disenfranchised and marginalized will remain marginalized and disenfranchised.

But in the end all of us will bear the burden of this marginalization, as communication studies will lack the resources to evolve and thereby achieve any relevance in a world that is increasingly diverse and faces many perilous scenarios. By reducing diversity to inclusion, what is lost is the fact that our popular communication theories lack the expansiveness to deal with the world that is now upon us, as well as the capacity to help us imagine the world in bold new ways. The struggle for diversity is ultimately a struggle for life.

CHAPTER 8

BEYOND INCLUSION

E pistemologically, ideologically, spiritually, and morally, I never found identity—in terms of race, ethnicity, gender, sexuality, and so forth—to be a heuristic construct. I have always struggled with what box to check. That is, which box can I fit into, or which box can contain *all* of my humanity, or which box can even begin to capture all of the ambiguity, complexity, and mystery that come with my own human experience? Practically and historically, I understand the need to pick a box. Resources, though often minimal, are often at stake. So I still choose the box that could materially benefit the most from my choice.

But I remain tortured by the process. It has nothing to do with my parents being of different races, or even my grandparents being from different corners of the world. It is about Audre Lorde and why liberation can only begin with the creation of new tools. Can identity build the house of the slave, and thereby be both a tool of the master and the slave? How could identity serve two fundamentally different causes, that of oppression and that of liberation? No doubt, the master needs a conception of identity that degrades our humanity. For what would be the possibility of slavery, apartheid,

Jim Crow practices, the Holocaust, and other such abominations without such an identity? But what did identity ever do for the slave? Why should the slave be bound by a conception of identity (this box business) that requires us to diminish all of our diversity, complexity, and, ultimately, our humanity? According to Cornell West, race matters, meaning identity matters. But for whom exactly, and for what purpose? Yes, as regards inclusion, identity matters. But when did the politics of inclusion become emancipatory, or the politics that best serves the cause of diversity? This, after all, is the same politics that created affirmative action to devalue, displace, and delegitimize reparations. So again, can the tools that build the house of the master also build the house of the slave?

Any rigorous and robust approach to framing and promoting diversity needs to acknowledge four key premises: (a) various peoples have been historically marginalized and disenfranchised, and the legacy of such discrimination and exclusion remains enduring; (b) dominant and prevailing institutional practices reflect and favor the ideological and material interests of various peoples, and thereby are inherently hostile to peoples of different interests; (c) as much as viewing diversity in terms of race, ethnicity, gender, sexuality, and disability is important, such a multicultural approach also masks and suppresses other kinds of diversity that are no less important, such as ideological diversity, epistemological diversity, pedagogical diversity, historical diversity, spiritual diversity, and existential diversity—that is, diversity in terms of being and knowing; (d) finally, all supposed expressions of diversity, and even claims of diversity, are by no means morally equal, meaning that only those ways of being and knowing that expand our limits of possibility genuinely qualify as diversity. Taking these premises seriously means looking diligently and critically at how our institutional norms and practices undercut diversity and, consequently, the entry and flourishing of perspectives that can be enriching and life affirming.

But all of this constitutes a different way of defining the struggle for diversity. Indeed, what happens when your own struggle for diversity is different, and even conflicts with the prevailing struggle for diversity? That is, what happens when you insist on viewing diversity in ways that exceed race, gender, sexual orientation, and disability, and thereby have no regards for any struggle for diversity that focuses on the inclusion and accommodation of differences? What also becomes of your own struggle for diversity when the status quo prefers to do business with the popular struggle for diversity, and is even able to use this struggle to undermine your own struggle? No doubt, after 350 years of slavery, Black Codes, and Jim Crow practices, race matters, and will long matter. Various peoples have been historically marginalized, disenfranchised, and brutalized, and this legacy has consequences and implications. These truths are real. But how did inclusion rather than revolution become the goal of the struggle for diversity and the best way to end our brutalizing of each other?

Viewing diversity in terms of inclusion assumes that various peoples were merely historically excluded for being different. Indeed, if such was the case, then inclusion is arguably a just solution. But African Americans, especially, were by no means merely excluded for being of a different race and/or ethnicity. For over 350 years, African Americans were enslaved, tortured, and brutalized. How could inclusion be a just solution for all of this misery? What also of our obligation to vanquish the epistemological practices that made for all this misery—that is, ending the tools that made for the building of the master's house? In my view, any rigorous struggle for diversity must reckon with understanding the origins of this misery and dismantling the epistemology that made for this misery. Viewing such misery racially uncomplicates our understanding of this misery. For even viewing persons in terms of race is an epistemological matter. But viewing diversity in terms of epistemology would make for a different struggle for diversity. It would mean looking at diversity in terms of being and knowing. It would also mean looking at diversity in terms of emancipation rather than inclusion.

There are many falsehoods at the core of our common understanding of the struggle for diversity that make impossible any redeeming of this enterprise. There is, again, the falsehood of identity, that our supposed identity (diversity) can be put neatly into boxes. In reality, any attempt to box our identity only diminishes our diversity and, ultimately, our humanity. There is the falsehood of equality, that inclusion promotes equality. If so, what to make of the widening gap between rich and poor in this age of diversity and inclusion? There is also the falsehood that diversity is about our differences. If so, what to make of our unwillingness to value, include, and celebrate those differences that culturally and religiously oppose our *chosen* differences? Then there is the falsehood of tolerance, as in the need to be civil to each other. This is civility functioning as a rhetorical apparatus to subjugate, discipline, and assimilate diversity. To invoke civility in the name of tolerance is to privilege our own sensibility. We are insidiously demanding that others share and even comply with our own sensibility. But the sharing of a common sensibility is homogeneity rather than diversity. If anything, diversity must at least mean that what I view as civil can be fundamentally different to what others view as civil. Thus why should I be rebuked and disciplined for refusing to comply and conform to your notion of civility? How did your definition of civility become so privileged as to possess the power to discipline other kinds of civility? Finally, there is the falsehood of inclusion, that inclusion and assimilation are good.

Diversity and inclusion discourses are always highlighting the supposed virtues of diversity and how promoting diversity makes for good business practice. Diversity is always encouraged to apply. However, the inclusion of diversity also means the assimilation of diversity. Diversity must conform to the norms, customs, and expectations of the status quo, meaning that inclusion involves accepting and even acknowledging the dominant paradigm as superior. The burden is on diversity to adapt to the status quo. This can mean meeting with your department chair upon your appointment and being given a five page document that explicitly and quantitatively lays out the publishing requirements for tenure and promotion, including a ranking of different scholarly journals. Gaining tenure and promotion depends on publishing in only the most prestigious journals, or what your department defines as prestigious. Inclusion means accepting these publishing demands as academic excellence. We must be ready to publish or perish like everyone else, regardless of race, creed, or gender. This is inclusion as assimilation. The onus is on diversity to conform and submit to a set of arbitrary standards that wants nothing to do with diversity. There can be no fundamental challenging of the status quo, such as engaging in modes of writing that are contrary to the norms of journal publishing, especially with regards those scholarly journals that are assumed to be the most prestigious. Any attempt to resist will usually result in rejection letters where anonymous peer reviews claim that your prose "lacks the specificity and precision that one associates with scholarly writing," the writing that is valued.

This valuing and privileging of "specificity and precision" is also why many of the most prestigious communication departments seek only candidates that employ quantitative research methods. These departments are assuming that communication is quantifiable. That communication is supposedly quantifiable means that communication can be measured and compared. In other words, quantitative methods can supposedly demystify communication.

In making communication quantifiable, such methods supposedly also make communication manipulable, thus reflecting and reinforcing our supposed ability to conquer human processes. In this way, quantitative methods supposedly allow us to bring the study of communication under our control, thereby supposedly allowing for specificity and precision in our claims. However, to believe that communication is quantifiable demands defining communication in ways that lend for quantification. This means defining communication as fundamentally a linguistic and symbolic activity. This is why definitions matter. Who defines "communication" controls what constitutes communication knowledge, who gets positions in prestigious communication departments, and what knowledge of communication is found in communication journals, textbooks, and curriculums.

"All is number," said Pythagoras, meaning that numbers have the ability to explain the workings of the world. Because we continue to believe this is true, we continue to perceive and make sense of everything through numbers. This is why we view diversity in terms of groups, labels, and boxes. We can put numbers to these things. This is also why we continue to view communication in terms of language and symbols. We can put numbers to these things. The moral of the story being that we make sense of things based on how we perceive them. So any view of diversity that has nothing to do with groups, labels, and boxes will be a problem for us. We are going to struggle to make sense of it. Just as well, any view of communication that emphasizes meaning is going to be a problem for us. There is nothing about meaning that is quantifiable. The reason being that meaning resides within and between human beings. The reason being that meaning is bound up with context, and context has many dimensions that are outside of our control. Finally, the reason being that meaning is bound up with life, so as our lives change, our meanings change. Meaning undermines our common notions of order. This is why inclusion wants would want nothing to do with it. For the first question that will arise is what does inclusion mean and to whom. Meaning would make everything open to scrutiny. Nothing will be off limits. There is simply no way that inclusion could wither the unrelenting scrutiny. Yet this is how meaning promotes human diversity. It exposes all the insidious forces and practices that block the rise of new meanings in the name of supposed noble causes like inclusion and civility.

Quantitative methods succeed by making the study of communication neat and tidy. This is accomplished by masking all the complexity, mystery, and diversity that surround the human experience. In fact, such methods can only work by reducing human diversity to groups, labels, and boxes. This is also why quantitative methods are so integral to preserving the status quo. Such methods reinforce our belief that human diversity resides in groups, labels, and boxes. In doing so, such methods help sustain a view of diversity that poses no threat to anything. This is also how a hegemon functions—different things working in tandem to maintain a certain order of things. In this case, quantitative methods promote a certain view of diversity that in turn promote and reinforce a certain view of communication.

Inclusion conspires to keep epistemology on the margins. To perpetuate a certain kind of scholarly writing is to perpetuate a certain way of understanding the world, relating to the world, embodying the world. In this case, to believe that scholarly writing should be about "specificity and precision" is to believe that the world lends for "specificity and precision" and that human beings are capable of achieving both from the world. However, many native and indigenous peoples throughout the world would claim that the world in no way lends for such "specificity and precision" and that it is our foolish pursuit of such "specificity and precision" that is responsible for all the harm and peril that is now upon the planet. Indeed, inclusion means limiting our attention to conceptual and methodological issues, such as bringing the experiences of minority peoples to dominant theories and methodologies. However, no theory or methodology comes out of a historical vacuum. In fact, no theory of knowledge comes out of a civilizational vacuum. Failing to look critically at the civilizational context from which our theories and methodologies are born impedes the struggle for diversity by encouraging us to miss the fact that producing new kinds of theories and methodologies is different to that of merely producing more theories and methodologies, and that new kinds of theories and methodologies can only come from new epistemologies.

To view diversity from the perspective of epistemology is to realize that disruption and revolution are necessary for the rise of diversity. Different epistemologies are like teutonic plates grinding against each other. Seismic and cataclysmic disruptions are inevitable, but also necessary for life's prosperity. The planet would be devoid of its boundless diversity without the violence that comes from these moving teutonic plates constantly grinding against each other. A false civility, one that seeks to coercively lessen the intensity and ferocity of our differences, impedes diversity. In an increasingly plural and multicultural world, collisions between different kinds of peoples are inevitable and necessary.

We continue to define diversity in terms of race, gender, sexual orientation, and disability, thereby helping to suppress the diversity found in our different rationalities, sensibilities, spiritualities, modalities, and epistemologies. Inclusion wants nothing to do with all of this diversity and complexity. Yet in helping the status quo masks all of this diversity and complexity, inclusion degrades our humanity. We are reduced to merely objects of inclusion who promise certain material rewards, like mentoring minority students. In reality, our exclusion of different peoples was fundamentally an epistemological matter. We did much more than exclude different kinds of peoples. We also enslaved, persecuted, brutalized, and killed different kinds of peoples. All this had to make sense to us. This is why epistemology matters. Epistemology is what shapes and guides how we make sense of things. Diversity and inclusion politics would have us believe that different peoples were merely excluded. Of course if such were the case, then inclusion makes sense. But because exclusion was never the original sin, then inclusion makes no sense. Indeed, what makes inclusion dangerous is that it never reaches the level of challenging the dominant epistemology, and thereby is complicit in keeping in place the epistemology that continues to make for the suffering and brutalizing of so many human beings.

Diversity and inclusion politics assumes that our goal should be to create a safe and nurturing space for diversity, one where diversity is valued, affirmed, and embraced. But diversity can only be included by being assimilated. In this way, inclusion degrades diversity, depoliticizes diversity, emasculates diversity. Inclusion strips diversity of diversity. In aiding and abetting the status quo in every which way, the common struggle for diversity becomes fully complicit in degrading diversity. In order for diversity to be diversity, neither inclusion nor assimilation can be viable options. Diversity must embrace all the tribulations that come with being marginalized and disenfranchised, harassed and forsaken. It must be ready to never enjoy the resources and privileges that come with being included and assimilated, such as Bayard Ruskin and Audre Lorde never being fully embraced by the Black community. It must also be ready to never have the safety and security that come with inclusion. Diversity must be ready to find the most creative and innovative ways to make do. But even on the margins, the status quo will demand that diversity enjoy no peace. There will always be incursions into the supposed badlands. So there will always be skirmishes. Diversity requires resolve and fortitude. We must be ready to endure and struggle.

Locating the Struggle

History is a story of conquest—peoples with superior means conquering other peoples with inferior means. As such, the knowledge that shapes the status quo is always of a nature that promotes and legitimizes conquest. Such are the spoils of conquest. Those who conquer get to impose a knowledge of conquest on other peoples. This story of history helps us to understand that knowledge is always situated within a civilizational context. Knowledge is always ideological and political. Those civilizations that rule the world do so by being able to impose a knowledge of conquest on the world. Therefore disrupting a knowledge system is no easy thing. The knowledge that forms the foundation of the sciences and disciplines in the western/European world is one that promotes and legitimizes conquest. At the core of this knowledge is the belief that the world is of an intractable conflict between supposedly positive and negative forces, such as order versus chaos, life versus death, mind versus body, meaning versus ambiguity, health versus disease, and so on. The mission of knowledge in a western/European context is to help us conquer and even vanquish the supposedly negative forces. This mission is prominent in our sciences and disciplines. In communication studies, the intractable conflict is supposedly between communication and confusion, meaning and ambiguity. What emerges is the notion of communication as a tool that involves precision and mastery. Such mastery will allow us to vanquish confusion and ambiguity. Communication courses focus on teaching us how to find "the available means of persuasion in any given situation." This means finding the most effective means to impose our own particular worldview on others so as to achieve our own self-interest. We come to view others as objects of persuasion and success is measured in our ability to command various skills and techniques that will allow our point of view to prevail. We also strive to produce theories and methodologies that will allow us to conquer and vanquish confusion and ambiguity. This is the knowledge found in communication textbooks and journals. This is also the knowledge we define and judge as important and excellent.

To look at the struggle for diversity from the level of epistemology in communication studies is to commit ourselves to building theories and methodologies that move us beyond conquest. Only by doing we can begin to write a new story of the human experience that saves us from the misery and loss of human diversity that come with the violence that conquest engenders. Building these new theories and methodologies is foremost an exercise in imagination. It is about reimagining what the world can be and how the study of communication can make for a new world that saves us from the ravages of conquest. This means doing teaching differently. Rather than focusing on learning and mastering the theories and methodologies that comprise the canon, now the focus needs to be on understanding the forces and experiences that limit our own ability to reimagine communication, and exploring different ways of releasing ourselves of these forces and experiences. It means posing questions like, "How can we begin to define and experience communication in ways that can fundamentally expand what you are capable of knowing and being? What would such a new definition of communication physically, emotionally, cognitively, and spiritually demand of us? What would such a definition mean for the world?"

Conclusion

Diversity is much more than merely different ways of perceiving the world. It is fundamentally about different ways of imagining and reimagining what the world can be. Any rigorous struggle for diversity should be about liberating and emancipating our imagination. Indeed, this is arguably the most serious problem with the common struggle for diversity. It degrades our conception of identity. We continue to view identity in terms of groups, labels, and boxes. But to view identity this way erases our diversity and complexity. It diminishes our humanity, and ultimately reflects a lack of moral and epistemological imagination, an unwillingness to look at the world anew. What remains is a status quo that continues to brutalize diversity by promoting conquest. It also makes people who have been historically marginalized and brutalized complicit in the oppression of diversity, such as civil rights leaders publicly condemning Martin Luther King Jr. for opposing the Vietnam war. The struggle for diversity becomes nothing but the oppression of diversity. A new conception of diversity implicates a new conception of identity. In my own case, I now define identity in terms of possibility because I define diversity as the affirmation of possibility. I view identity as a conceptual space, a space of possibility. It is a space where I imagine and explore new ways of being in the world. I am committed to the nurturing of this space, and also to furnishing this space with all the relational and epistemological resources I need. It is the cultivation and protection of these kinds of spaces that I view as the struggle for diversity.

EPILOGUE

When you hear or read my words, you would do well to always remember that you are *really* interpreting my words, and doing so from a certain racial, cultural, emotional, spiritual, existential, and intellectual perspective that is most likely fundamentally different from mine. The meaning you are deriving from my words is merely *your* meaning. You should never assume that you know definitively the meaning I intend, and neither should I assume that my own meaning is obvious to you. In order for communication to rise and flourish, humility and restraint are vital. Both serve us well in terms of lessening tension and conflict.

Just as much as you are entitled to your interpretation, just as much I am entitled to my intent. That you are judging my words to be offensive, only means that you are interpreting my words to be so. In communication, my intention and your interpretation should both matter. This means that I should always be conscious of the fact that my own words can always lend for different interpretations, and that my own interpretation of the words of others should always remain vulnerable to the intention of others. We should therefore always interpret the words of others kindly and gently.

This is how communication makes us beautiful, meaning this is how communication cultivates the best in us. When communication becomes possible, we become beautiful. This is also how communication saves us from violence and strife. Also, in order for communication to flourish, both intention and interpretation must remain in tension with each other. This is how vulnerability becomes foundational to communication. Without vulnerability, as in I refusing to be vulnerable to your interpretation, and you refusing to be vulnerable to my intention, communication is impossible. So with regards what becomes of us, communication matters.

We are supposedly now in the age of difference. We are supposedly now all valuing difference, embracing difference, celebrating difference, bridging difference, accommodating difference, including difference. However, nearly all of this embracing and including of difference is coming from a place that is hostile to doubt. There is no allowing for a different perspective, a different interpretation, a different reality, a different truth. We get a difference that is militant and strident, cruel and vindictive, obnoxious and self-rightous. This difference wants nothing to do with communication. It prefers to condemn and threaten. It will tolerate no dissent. Yet this is also the irony—this difference will tolerate no difference. How then is this intolerance of difference any different from any other intolerance of difference? Yet this is the difference we are now to embrace for the sake of inclusion. It claims to value diversity but wants conformity in the end. What then is the value of this difference?

We need a new politics of difference. We need to release difference from race, gender, ethnicity, and sexuality. In various contexts these kinds of differences no doubt matter. However, that a person is racially, biologically, or sexually different in no way means that the person is intellectually different, epistemologically different, politically different, ethically different, culturally different, ideologically different, or even spiritually different. In short, a person being different in no way means that the person is truly different.

To value difference is to value what difference promises—the possibility to disrupt the status quo by creating something that can enlarge our sense of possibility. However, in order for difference to do this, it must cultivate doubt. Doubt is the engine room of difference. In promoting vulnerability, doubt lends for possibility. Without doubt, and especially the embracing of doubt, difference means nothing. It loses its power and fecundity.

Finally, we need to release difference from inclusion. The only way to include difference is by normalizing difference, pacifying difference, assimilating difference. However, difference must always pose a threat to the status quo, which means that it must always be in tension with what we commonly believe and value. It must always be fomenting doubt and confusion. This is how difference succeeds, by making us vulnerable to possibility. In other words, difference succeeds by challenging us to question everything we believe and value. This is why there can be no inclusion of difference. For why would any system of power and privilege embrace forces that contain the possibility of its own demise? As such, difference will always face defamation, persecution, and exclusion. Such is the reality of difference. However, to recognize that doubt is inevitable is to recognize that difference is also inevitable. There is always the possibility of a different perspective, a different truth, a different interpretation, a different reality. This is how difference renews the world. This is how difference affirms life.

REFERENCES

Alston, K. (1998). Hands off consensual sex. *Academe, 84,* 32-33.

Asher, L. (2018, April 29). How ed schools became a menace. *Chronicle of Higher Education.* https://www.chronicle.com/article/How-Ed-Schools-Became-a-Menace/243062

Aurelius, M. (2006). *Meditations.* New York: Penguin Books.

Baker, J. B., & Shao, L. X. (2013). The normativity of using prison to control hate speech: The hollowness of Waldron's harm theory. *New Criminal Law Review, 16,* 621-656.

Bejan, T. (2017). *Mere civility: Disagreement and the limits of toleration.* Cambridge, MA: Harvard University Press.

Bellas, M. L., & Gossett, J. L. (2001). Love or the "lecherous professor": Consensual relationships between professors and students. *Sociological Quarterly, 42,* 529-558.

Brewer, E., & Westerman, J. (2018). *Organizational Communication: Today's Professional Life in Context.* New York. Oxford University Press.

Conquergood, D. (2002). Performance studies: Interventions and radical research. *The Drama Review, 42 (2),* 145-156.

Cooper, P. J., Calloway-Thomas, C., & Simonds, C. J. (2007). *Intercultural communication: A text with readings.* Boston, MA: Pearson.

Dennett, D. C. (1994). The role of language in intelligence. In Jean Khalfa (Ed.), *What is Intelligence?: The Darwin College Lectures* (pp. 161-178). Cambridge: Cambridge University Press.

Dyson, M. E. (2018). *What Truth Sounds Like: RFK, James Baldwin, and our Unfinished Conversation about Race in America.* New York: St. Martin's Press.

Fassett, D. L., Warren, J. T., & Nainby, K. (2018). *Communication: A Critical/Cultural Introduction.* San Diego, CA: Cognella.

Gerbner, G. (1974). Communication: Society is the message. *Communication, 1,* 57-66.

Ginsberg, B. (2011). *The fall of the Faculty: The rise of the All-Administrative University and why it matters.* New York: Oxford University Press.

Gudykunst, W. B., & Kim, Y. Y. (2003). *Communication with strangers: An approach to intercultural communication.* Boston, MA: McGraw-Hill.

Haney, C. (2009). *Reforming punishment: Psychological limits to the pains of imprisonment.* Washington, DC: American Psychological Association.

Hechinger Report (November 17, 2016). *As college costs rise, so do the number of administrators: Why the ranks of bureaucrats on campus continues to increase.* https://hechingerreport.org/college-costs-rise-number-administrators/

Hicks, D. (2018). *Leading with dignity: How to create a culture that brings out the best in people.* New Haven: Yale University Press.

Johnson, M. (2007). *The meaning of the body: Aesthetics of human understanding.* Chicago, IL: University of Chicago Press.

Jones, P. (2015). Dignity, hate and harm. *Political Theory, 43,* 678-686.

Klopf, D. W., & McCroskey, J. C. (2007). *Intercultural communication encounters.* Boston, MA: Pearson.

Lepore, J. (2017, October 9). Inquietude. *New Yorker.*

Lillienfeld, S. O. (2017). Microaggressions: Strong claims, inadequate evidence. *Perspectives on Psychological Science, 12,* 138-169.

Lingis, A. (1994). *The community of those who have nothing in common.* Bloomington, IN: Indiana University Press.

Littlejohn, S. W. (1996). *Theories of Human Communication* (5th Edition). Belmont, CA: Wadsworth.

Marantz, A. (2018, July 2). Fighting words: The far right tests free speech on campus. *New Yorker.*

Martin, J. N., & Nakayama, T. K. (2007). *Intercultural communication in contexts.* Boston, MA: McGraw-Hill.

McArthur, N. (2017). Relationships between university professors and students: Should they be banned? *Ethics and Education, 12,* 129-140.

Morris, P. (Ed.) (1994). *The Bakhtin Reader: Selected Writings of Bakhtin, Medvedev, Voloshinov.* New York: Oxford University Press.

Neuliep, J. W. (2015). *Intercultural communication: A Contextual Approach.* Thousand Oaks, CA: Sage.

Neuliep, J. W. (2000). *Intercultural communication: A contextual approach.* Boston, MA: Houghton Mifflin.

Newman, S. L. (2017). Finding the harm in hate speech: An argument against censorship. *Canadian Journal of Political Science, 50,* 679-697.

Postman, N. (1979). *Teaching as a Conserving Activity.* New York: Dell.

Richmond, V. P., & McCroskey, J. C. (2009). *Organizational communication for survival.* Boston: Pearson.

Rogers, E. M., & Steinfatt, T. M. (1999). *Intercultural communication.* Prospect Heights, IL: Waveland.

Samovar, L. A., Porter, R. E., & McDaniel, E. R. (2006). *Intercultural communication.* Belmont, CA: Thomson Wadsworth.

Samovar, L. A., Porter, R. E., & McDaniel, E. R. (2007). *Communication between cultures.* Belmont, CA: Thomson Wadsworth.

Skeen, R., & Nielsen, J. (1983). Student-faculty sexual relationships: An empirical test of two explanatory models. *Qualitative Sociology, 6,* 99-117.

Steinberg, S. (2006). *Introduction to communication.* Cape Town: Juta.

Thayer, L. (2011). *Explaining things: Inventing ourselves and our worlds.* New York: Xlibris.

Thayer, L. (1987). *On Communication: Essays in Understanding.* Norwood, NJ: Ablex Press.

Waldron, J. (2012a). *The harm in hate speech.* Cambridge, MA: Harvard University Press.

Waldron, J. (2012b, June 18). Hate speech and free speech, part two. *New York Times* https://opinionator.blogs.nytimes.com/2012/06/18/hate-speech-and-free-speech-part-two/

ABOUT THE AUTHOR

Amardo Rodriguez (Ph.D., Howard University) is a Laura J. and L. Douglas Meredith Professor in the Department of Communication and Rhetorical Studies at Syracuse University. His research interest is in postcolonial theory, specifically in postcolonizing communication studies. His most recent book-length monographs, *Communication: Colonization and the Making of Discipline* and *Notes From The Margins: Reflections on Regimes of Knowledge and Power*, were published by Public Square Press. He has also published papers in such journals as, *Journal of Race & Policy*, *Journal of Latino/Latin American Studies*, *Cultural Studies/Critical Methodologies*, *Postcolonial Studies*, and the *International Journal of Discrimination and the Law*. Prof. Rodriguez teaches in areas related to communication theory and inquiry.